SPELLING FOR ADULTS

SPELLING FOR ADULTS

CHARLES W. RYAN

John Wiley & Sons, Inc.

New York · London · Sydney · Toronto

Library of Congress Cataloging in Publication Data

Ryan, Charles William, 1932-
    Spelling for adults.

    (Wiley self-teaching guides)
    1.   English language—Orthography and spelling—
Programmed instruction.   I.   Title.
(PE1145.4.R9)   428'.1   73-5831
ISBN 0-471-74788-2

Printed in the United States of America

73   74   10 9 8 7 6 5 4 3 2 1

To Mother. What one cannot repay,
one can still acknowledge.

To the Reader

Everyone is talking about "communication" these days. The word is so overused that a "breakdown in communication" is often meant to excuse rather than to explain. But good communication is of vital importance.

Consider two ways of expressing the same idea:

> I ain't never recieved an anser from your office in Pitsburg.

> I have never received an answer from your office in Pittsburgh.

Each of these sentences communicates exactly the same idea about the failure to receive a response from Pittsburgh; however, one is written in "Standard English" while the other is not. The striking difference between the two ways of writing the same thing lies in the reader's image of the writer.

You are judged, often harshly, by your command of the spoken and written language. If you can improve your ability to express yourself in writing, the practical advantages are obvious—including the greater self-confidence you feel when you write.

A great many errors in spelling stem from the fact that people never really see the words. The ability to focus attention on the words themselves can be developed. The basic objective of this book is to help you improve your spelling through discussion and exercises that will get you involved in the structure of words.

Several years ago I took up oil painting as a hobby. After only a short time, I was amazed at the difference in the way I looked at the world around me. Where once I would see a hill, green with grass, and think I had seen all there was to see about that hill, I arrived at a stage where I could see the same hill with all its variations of light and shadow and changing shades of green. I did not become a very good painter, but I did develop an ability to see the world around me as I had never seen it before.

My basic approach in this book is to try to help you see words in terms of their structure. Rules are discussed with the idea that if you can understand the reason for a rule—even though there are exceptions and the rule might not be entirely logical—you will be able to apply it more effectively.

I have tried to isolate some of the major causes of spelling problems, using examples of words in each category that illustrate the approach toward solving the problem. You are given the opportunity, through in-text exercises, to participate in the problem-solving, checking your progress as you go. Sometimes, lists of the principal words of a particular structure are provided. These are furnished not only to provide a ready reference list of the words correctly spelled but also to give you material with which you may work out the relationships that are useful for you.

I don't pretend that I have provided solutions for all your spelling problems. I do believe, however, that if you study this book, preferably at regular intervals, you can greatly improve your ability to spell correctly.

Pacific Grove, California   Charles W. Ryan
September, 1973

How to Use This Book

Much of the material in this book is in the form of programmed instruction, a technique that helps you learn more effectively by getting you directly involved in the material. Each bit (or frame) of programmed material is numbered. Have a pencil and an index card (or folded piece of paper) ready. When you reach a numbered frame, use the card to cover the answer below the dashed line. Read the question or instruction, do what is asked for in the frame, and then check your answer. If you are correct, go ahead. If you make a mistake, be sure you understand the reason for your error before you go on.

Not everyone has the same problems with spelling. Some of the material may seem too easy, but you will progress rapidly through these easy or familiar sections. When you reach sections that deal with your particular problems, slow down to make sure you thoroughly understand the material presented.

Part 4 offers supplemental material for those who wish even further guidance in learning to spell. The Appendix includes additional lists of words, grouped by occupation.

Each chapter ends with a Self-Test to help you evaluate your mastery of the concepts presented. Before going on to the next chapter, take this test, check your answers, and review the chapter if you missed many items. A Final Test is also included (in Chapter 21), along with answers.

Contents

Introduction	THE WORD BOOK	1
	Use of the Dictionary	
PART 1		3
Chapter 1	THE LONG AND THE SHORT OF IT	4
	The Silent E	
Chapter 2	WHEN TO DROP A LETTER	14
	Problems with Endings	
Chapter 3	DOUBLE TROUBLE	22
	When to Double a Consonant	
Chapter 4	THE SOUNDS OF C, G, AND S	34
	Hard and Soft Sounds of These Consonants	
PART 2		49
Chapter 5	FINAL Y: EASY AS PIE	50
Chapter 6	THE NOT-SO-SIMPLE PLURALS	53
Chapter 7	THE LONG VOWEL SOUNDS	69
	Vowel Combinations to Indicate Long Vowel Sounds	
Chapter 8	"EXCEPT AFTER C"	75
	Problems with ie and ei	
Chapter 9	SH-H-H!	80
	Spelling the Sound of sh	

Chapter 10 THE LETTER SAVER   86

          Dealing with the Apostrophe

Chapter 11 BEGINNINGS   90

          Problems with Prefixes

Part 3   105

Chapter 12 THE QUANDARY ABOUT -ARY AND -ERY   106

Chapter 13 TROUBLE WITH -ABLE AND -IBLE   111

Chapter 14 SIZE UP -IZE, -YZE, AND -ISE   125

Chapter 15 GRIEVOUS SINS, MISCHIEVOUS PRANKS,
          AND HEINOUS CRIMES   129

          Problems with -ious, -eous, -ous, -ius,
          and -us

Chapter 16 MAKE THE CONNECTION BETWEEN -SION
          AND -TION   135

Chapter 17 THE ANT AND THE ENT   141

          Problems with -ant, -ent, -ance, -ence,
          -ancy, and -ency

Chapter 18 IDENTIFY -IFY AND -EFY   149

Chapter 19 THE BUTCHER, THE ACTOR, AND THE
          CANDLESTICK MAKER   152

          Problems with -er, -or, -eer, -ier,
          -eur, and -euse

Chapter 20 EXCEED YOUR GOAL AND PROCEED TO
          SUCCEED   156

          Problems with -ceed, -cede, and -sede

Chapter 21 THE RECKONING   160

          Final Examination

PART 4   175

   Supplement 1 FOILED BY MISPRONUNCIATION   176

   Supplement 2 SILENT BEGINNINGS   179

   Supplement 3 TROUBLESOME TWINS   182

   Supplement 4 NO FUN WITH THE FRENCH   197

   Supplement 5 GRAPPLING WITH GERMAN   200

   Supplement 6 SPELLING IN SPANISH   202

   Supplement 7 DO-IT-YOURSELF MEMORY AIDS   204

APPENDIX   SOME SPECIAL WORD LISTS   206

SPELLING FOR ADULTS

INTRODUCTION

The Word Book

The Scandinavians call it a "word book" and the Germans, a "word treasure." Our own word for it is less colorful, but at least "dictionary" implies the importance of the sounds of words. If you are serious about improving your spelling (and you probably are if you paid good money for this book), you should form the habit of looking up words in the dictionary.

First of all, a dictionary shows you how a word is spelled—that is, if you can find it. Of course, you can get the first letter right most of the time. (You may have a little trouble with words like PNEUMONIA, PSYCHOLOGY, GNOME, OR PTARMIGAN, which have silent initial letters. Supplement 2 in Part 4 will give you some help with these.) If your first guess about the initial letter happens to be wrong, don't give up. Look under alternate spellings until you find the word you're after.

Suppose you want to look up CHARACTER, which sounds as if it begins with a k, but a search under the k's does not reveal the word. Then you remember that c often has the sound of k. Since the second letter is probably a, you look through the words beginning with ca. It's not there. Just as you are about to decide that somehow the word was left out of the dictionary, you remember that CHRISTMAS begins with ch, so maybe CHARACTER does, too. And you're right!

Take another example. In looking up the spelling of CHARADE, you naturally start with the sh words, but without success. You know that CHEVROLET begins with the sound of sh, so you look in that section of the dictionary, and there's your word.

Consider still another word. You are not sure how GESTURE is spelled, and a search under the j's does not help. You know that g in the spoken alphabet begins with a j sound, and your second try, under the g's, locates the word.

Next, the dictionary shows you how a word is pronounced, which is very helpful in learning to spell correctly. The dictionary uses little symbols (called diacritical marks) over the vowels to indicate the sounds.

In this book we'll use just the two marks for long or short vowels. Many of the guidelines in this book will help you make the connection between pronunciation and spelling.

Most dictionaries also give the <u>derivation</u> (or the history) of words. The English language is the richest language in the world because words from most of the world's languages have found their way into ours. The science that deals with the history of words is called etymology, and <u>that</u> word comes from the Greek <u>etymologia</u>, which means the same thing.

Finally, a word of caution. You haven't finished looking up the spelling of a word until you check the meaning of the word. Many English words sound alike but mean different things, while others are spelled alike but do not sound alike. So check the definition to be sure the word you have found is the right one!

Part One

This part focuses on the effects of the letter e. An e at the end of a word is often silent and unnoticed—but it is the key to many people's spelling problems. When you complete this section, you should be able to:

- identify long and short vowels;

- add the silent e at the end of appropriate words;

- recognize incorrect spellings and correctly spell words following the silent e rule;

- drop the silent e when appropriate before adding an ending to a basic word;

- double a letter within a word when appropriate according to the silent e rule;

- recognize the effect of the silent e on a preceding c, g, or s and modify the spelling accordingly;

- distinguish between the hard and soft sounds of c, g, and s.

Of course, spelling is not like mathematics—its rules are far from absolute. But the general guidelines you learn here will help you solve many troublesome spelling problems.

CHAPTER 1

The Long and the Short of It

Most of the twenty-six letters of the alphabet are consonants, but the letters used most often and which provide most of the basic sounds of the language are the vowels. For many people the key to good spelling is distinguishing between long vowels and short vowels.

1. Five letters of the alphabet are <u>always</u> vowels. Say them aloud as you write them. _____

- - - - - - - - - - - - - - - -

a, e, i, o, u

Note: Two other letters, <u>w</u> and <u>y</u>, are sometimes vowels. In words like TRY and EVERY, <u>y</u> is a vowel, but <u>w</u> is never a vowel unless it is used in combination with another vowel in words like OWL and SHAWL.

2. A long vowel is one that sounds the way it does when said in the alphabet. (That's not precisely true of <u>u</u>, but it's close enough.) A straight horizontal line over the vowel indicates that it is long. Some examples of words with long vowels are lāte, Pēte, bīte, hōse, and tūne. Mark each vowel below to show the long sound:

a   e   i   o   u

- - - - - - - - - - - - - - - -

ā   ē   ī   ō   ū

3. A short vowel is indicated by a symbol that looks almost like a small <u>o</u> with the upper half chopped off. Some examples of words with short vowels are: căt, bĕt, ĭs, sŏd, and fŭn. Mark each vowel below to show the short sound:

a   e   i   o   u

- - - - - - - - - - - - - - -
ă   ĕ   ĭ   ŏ   ŭ

4. Probably one of the first words you learned how to spell was RAT. Mark the vowel to give it the proper sound (short a̲):

      rat

- - - - - - - - - - - - - - -
  răt

5. Now mark the vowel to indicate the sound of long a̲:

      rat

- - - - - - - - - - - - - - -
  rāt

6. What real word (although it is spelled differently) sounds exactly like rāt? _____

- - - - - - - - - - - - - - -
    rate

7. Below are five words written as they might appear in a dictionary to show pronunciation. How are they normally written?

(a) lāt _____   (d) hōz _____

(b) pēt _____   (e) tūn _____

(c) bīt _____

- - - - - - - - - - - - - - -
    (a) late; (b) Pete; (c) bite; (d) hose; (e) tune

Note: If you wrote PEAT instead of PETE for (b) you are still correct, but you have happened upon another subject that we will deal with in Chapter 7.

8. Notice that all five words in frame 7 end with a vowel that has no sound at all—the silent e. That is what this chapter is really about, as you will see.

All the vowels in the following group of words are either long, short, or silent. Mark all the sounded vowels to show the long and short sounds, and underline the silent vowels.

Sam   tin   rum   fate   cane   writ   mete   fat   rob   cute

scene   can   tine   scent   stun   dote   same   met   bed   fume

tome   robe   Tom   cut   rid   impede   write   dot   ride   tune

— — — — — — — — — — — —

Săm   tĭn   rŭm   fāte   cāne   wrĭt   mēte   făt   rŏb   cūte

scēne   căn   tīne   scĕnt   stŭn   dōte   sāme   mĕt   bĕd   fūme

tōme   rōbe   Tŏm   cŭt   rĭd   ĭmpēde   wrīte   dŏt   rīde   tūne

Note: WRIT and WRITE have silent first letters. See Part 4, Supplement 2.

9. Look at the group of words in frame 8 again. Only one of them has all three kinds of vowels—long, short, and silent. Which word is it?

——————————————

— — — — — — — — — — — —

    impede

10. The words from frame 8 are rearranged below into separate groups with the short vowel sounds in one column and the long vowel sounds in the other. (IMPEDE has one of each vowel sound, but the accented vowel is long, so it goes in the second column.)

Short Vowels	Long Vowels
Sam, fat, can	same, fate, cane
bed, met, scent	impede, mete,* scene
rid, writ, tin	ride, write, tine
rob, dot, Tom	robe, dote, tome
stun, cut, rum	tune, cute, fume

All the silent e's ended up in the same group. Which group?

——————————————

——————

*If METE is an unfamiliar word, look it up in the dictionary. It is not the present tense of MET.

- - - - - - - - - - - - - -

long vowels

11. You might have observed that the silent e at the end of a word "changes" the <u>preceding</u> vowel sound from short to long. (This is the silent e rule.) Let's look at a few of the words again:

făt	fāte
mĕt	mēte
wrĭt	wrīte
dŏt	dōte
cŭt	cūte

Use arrows and the marks for long and short vowel sounds to show how the silent e affects the sound of the preceding vowel in the following words:

Sam   tine   tune   ride   rum

stun   scene   can   robe   cane

- - - - - - - - - - - - - -

Săm   tīne   tūne   rīde   rŭm

stŭn   scēne   căn   rōbe   cāne

This is a good place to take a break. If you don't stop here, continue to the end of the chapter.

12. So far we have dealt with one-syllable words, but the silent e̲ operates in the same way with longer words, such as IMPEDE. In fact, longer words will give you less spelling trouble if you break them into parts (as we will be doing throughout the book) and apply the silent e̲ rule wherever appropriate.

In the following group of words, mark all the <u>sounded</u> vowels to show the long and short sounds, and underline the silent e̲'s.

hesitate   obscene   contrive   explode   solitude

pavement   supersede   asinine   intone   destitute

parade   obese   deposit   develop   parachute

- - - - - - - - - - - - - - -

hĕsĭtāte̲   ŏbscēne̲   cŏntrīve̲   ĕxplōde̲   sŏlĭtūde̲

pāvemĕnt   sūpĕrsēde̲   ăsĭnīne̲   ĭntōne̲   dĕstĭtūte̲

părāde̲   ōbēse̲   dēpŏsĭt   dēvĕlŏp   părăchūte̲

Note: Silent e̲ distinguishes between the long and short sounds of a <u>single</u> vowel followed by a <u>single</u> consonant, as in PET and PETE. It is <u>not</u> used when a long vowel sound is indicated in another way, as in PEAT (see Chapter 7), or when the word ends with more than one consonant, as in PE<u>ST</u>.

13. So far we have concentrated on how the silent e̲ affects the pronunciation of vowels in words. However, the problem with spelling is the other way around—you know how to <u>say</u> it, but you don't know how to <u>write</u> it. The next few frames will give you some practice in going from the spoken to the written word. Think about the silent e̲ as you answer.

When you finish a job, you com_____ it.

- - - - - - - - - - - - - - -

complete

14. When you give a description of something, you _____ it.

- - - - - - - - - - - - - - -

describe

15. When bears go to sleep for the winter, they hiber_____.

- - - - - - - - - - - - - - -

    hibernate

16. A crazy person is one who is ins_____.

- - - - - - - - - - - - - - -

    insane

17. After a photographer takes his pictures, he has to dev_____
the film in the darkroom.

- - - - - - - - - - - - - - -

    develop

18. A lighted sign over the door in a theatre marks the ex_____.

- - - - - - - - - - - - - - -

    exit

19. People with certain heart ailments should avoid undue

exc_____ment.

- - - - - - - - - - - - - - -

    excitement

20. Circle every misspelled word in the following sentence and correct
the spelling:

      A shope in Clevland wrot me to dune me for an overdue

      bill, but I replied that they had made a mistak in the billing.

- - - - - - - - - - - - - - -

    shop, Cleveland, wrote, dun, mistake

There is much more to learn about the e in our language, and the
more you know about that little letter, the easier it will be for you to
learn to spell correctly. (Printers and typesetters sometimes refer to
a little gremlin of the printing trade called Etaoin Shrdlu. The name
comes from the fact that those letters—e, t, a, o, i, n, s, h, r, d, l,
and u—are the most frequently used in the language, with e occurring
most often.)

You will not be surprised to learn that there are exceptions to the silent e rule. Consider the Mother Goose rhyme about that poor old lady and her dog:

> Old Mother Hubbard
>   Went to the cupboard
> To fetch her poor dog a bone;
>   But when she got there
> The cupboard was bare,
>   And so the poor dog had none.

Everyone knows, of course, that NONE does not rhyme with BONE, but it did when the rhyme was written. Often the common words in a language change most because they are used most. (Even by the time of Mother Goose, CUPBOARD no longer sounded like CUP BOARD.) But because everyday words are used so much, you probably won't have much trouble spelling them, rule or no rule.

Here are some of the common words that refuse to follow the silent e rule:

come   some   were   are   done

A word of caution is in order here. Very common words are not the only exceptions to the silent e rule. The usual rule is followed, for example, in SPITE, but the accent is shifted to another syllable in the related word RES´PITE (pronounced with a short i). Other words with a short i, because of the shift of accent, are IN´FI NITE and DEF´I NITE. (Other affects of accent shifts are discussed in Chapter 3.) In several other words, the silent e is retained for reasons that are beyond the scope of this chapter.

Some of the words in which the vowel preceding the silent e is not long are:

practice	service	novice
composite	opposite	gasoline

If you are beginning to suspect that most of the exceptions to the silent e rule involve the letter i, you are right! Try your hand at the following exceptions.

21. The Governor was nominated by the delegation from his state as a

nat_____ son candidate.

- - - - - - - - - - - - - -

native

22. She refused her husband's offer to do the dishes because she was
afraid he would break her frag_____ crystal.

_ _ _ _ _ _ _ _ _ _ _ _ _ _ _

    fragile

23. The famous designer's new line of gowns included items of
superla_____ beauty and quality; in short, they were the
ultim_____ in high fashion.

_ _ _ _ _ _ _ _ _ _ _ _ _ _ _

    superlative, ultimate

24. Rocks are made of many mineral substances, including agate, lime-
stone, and gran_____.

_ _ _ _ _ _ _ _ _ _ _ _ _ _ _

    granite

25. To review: The silent e, following a single consonant, gives the
preceding vowel a _____ sound.
                        (long/short)

_ _ _ _ _ _ _ _ _ _ _ _ _ _ _

    long

26. When a word ends with a single consonant, a single vowel immedi-
ately preceding the consonant is _____.
                             (long/short)

_ _ _ _ _ _ _ _ _ _ _ _ _ _ _

    short

27. The i in ADJECTIVE is not long, despite the silent e, because the
syllable containing it is _____.
                        (accented/unaccented)

_ _ _ _ _ _ _ _ _ _ _ _ _ _ _

    unaccented

The basic silent e rule remains in effect when some other letter is added, as in:

late, later   devote, devoted   plane, planes

Of course, the e might not be silent after the other letters are added! More about this in later chapters, especially Chapter 3, which deals with doubling consonants.

SELF-TEST

Circle each word below that is misspelled and write the correct spelling in the space beside it.

1. granit	_____	9. definite	_____
2. decide	_____	10. scrub	_____
3. hesitat	_____	11. bewar	_____
4. devoted	_____	12. compete	_____
5. drope	_____	13. skin	_____
6. began	_____	14. regrete	_____
7. likness	_____	15. airplan	_____
8. introduce	_____	16. blote	_____

ANSWERS TO SELF-TEST

1. granite	11.	beware
3. hesitate	14.	regret
5. drop	15.	airplane
7. likeness	16.	blot

All other words are spelled correctly.

Note: If you spelled the last word BLOAT, you are also correct; you applied the silent e rule to come up with the sound of a real word. See Chapter 7 for vowel combinations that indicate long vowel sounds.

CHAPTER 2

When to Drop a Letter

An ending is frequently added to a basic word to form a longer related word.   Some examples of such endings are -er in LONGER, -est in SMALLEST, -ed in WANTED, -ing in BURNING, -es in CATCHES, -ly in MANLY, -hood in CHILDHOOD, -ness in KINDNESS, and -ment in DEVELOPMENT. All these examples present no problem in spelling because the basic words end in consonants and the ending is simply added to the word.

1. The _____ _____
              (one who SURFS)   (past of WAIT)

_____ly to catch a big wave.
  (form of PATIENT)

- - - - - - - - - - - - -

   surfer, waited, patiently

   Caution: Sometimes the final consonant is doubled, as in BIG, BIGGER; DROP, DROPPED. Such words follow a different rule, which is discussed in Chapter 3.

2. What if the basic word ends in silent e? Do you keep the e or drop it? There is still no problem if the ending starts with e, as in LARGER, RIPEST, and HOPED, because experience since childhood has taught you that there is no double e in such longer word forms.

   The landscap_____ was not_____ for the fin_____ arrange-
             (-er)   (-ed)   (-est)
ments of shrubs and flowers in the area.

- - - - - - - - - - - - -

   landscaper, noted, finest

3. With very few exceptions (which will be discussed later in the chapter) there is no problem if the ending starts with a consonant (as in LIKELY, WORKMANSHIP, HEALTHFUL, and USELESS). The basic word is unchanged and the ending is simply added to the word.

The City Planning Commission was _____ful to hold
(form of CARE)

public hearings before approving the new housing develop_____.

– – – – – – – – – – – – – –

careful, development

4. The basic word _____ changed before adding an ending that
(is/is not)
starts with a consonant.

– – – – – – – – – – – – – –

is not

5. The main problems with endings arise when the ending begins with a vowel other than e. Some of these endings are: -al, -ic, -ice, -ure, -ing, -ance, -ory, -able, and -ary. Study the following words:

base, basic	enclose, enclosure
advise, advisory	guide, guiding, guidance[*]
desire, desirable[*]	continue, continual
tribute, tributary[*]	serve, service

Circle each word in the following sentence that is formed from a basic word ending in e and an ending starting with a vowel:

Making use of the law of supply and demand in distributing

goods and services is a basic element of modern capitalism.

– – – – – – – – – – – – – –

making (make), distributing (distribute), services (serve), basic (base)

Note: CAPITALISM has an ending that starts with a vowel, but the basic word CAPITAL does not end in e.

---

* The endings -able and -ible are discussed in Chapter 13, -ary and -ery in Chapter 12, and -ance and -ence in Chapter 17.

6.   Following the pattern of the examples given in frame 5, complete the following:

Japan, "the land of the _____ sun," has become
                        (form of RISE)

_____ in _____ industry and
   (form of SUCCESS)   (form of DEVELOP)

technology while _____ a fine
                       (form of PRESERVE)

_____al tradition.
   (form of CULTURE)

– – – – – – – – – – – – – – –

   rising, successful, developing, preserving, cultural

7.   The Prune _____ory Board ran a series of
                      (form of ADVISE)

_____ commercials.
   (form of AMUSE)

– – – – – – – – – – – – – – –

   Advisory, amusing

8.   From the examples given in frames 5-7, complete this general rule:
When an ending that starts with a vowel is added to a basic word ending

in e, the e is usually _____.
                            (dropped/retained)

– – – – – – – – – – – – – – –

   dropped

9.   When the e is not dropped, there is usually a good reason for keeping
it. The -ing form of SING is SINGING, but the -ing form of TINGE is
TINGEING because dropping the e would produce a word that rhymes with
RINGING.

   The -ing form of SINGE is _____.

– – – – – – – – – – – – – – –

   singeing

10. Sometimes the e is retained before the ending to distinguish between similar words, such as DIE and DYE. Since the -ing form of DIE is

DYING, the -ing form of DYE is _____ .

— — — — — — — — — — — — — — —

    dyeing

11. Here are some other exceptions to the rule that the e is dropped before adding an ending that starts with a vowel:

advantage, advantageous	mile, mileage
agree, agreeable	notice, noticeable
change, changeable	plebe, plebeian
manage, manageable	service, serviceable

Many of the above exceptions involve the letters c or g; these words follow another rule which is discussed in Chapter 4.

    The lawyer knew it would be _____ to establish
                             (form of ADVANTAGE)

that the written _____ was not _____
                 (form of AGREE)   (form of ENFORCE)

under the law.

— — — — — — — — — — — — — — —

    advantageous, agreement, enforceable

12. We discovered with little _____ that the
                          (form of PLEASE)

_____ weather was not _____ satis-
  (form of CHANGE)   (form of ENTIRE)

factory for a picnic.

— — — — — — — — — — — — — — —

    pleasure, changeable, entirely

13. The new method of _____ the fabric had a
                (form of DYE)

_____ effect on its final cost.
(form of NOTICE)

— — — — — — — — — — — — — — —

    dyeing, noticeable

14.   There are also some exceptions to the rule that the final e̱ is retained before adding an ending that starts with a consonant. Two important exceptions to this rule are the basic words ACKNOWLEDGE and
JUDGE. The e̱ is dropped from both words before adding -ment.
     The -ment form of JUDGE is JUDGMENT. The -ment form of

ACKNOWLEDGE is _____.

_ _ _ _ _ _ _ _ _ _ _ _ _ _

     acknowledgment

     Note: The dictionary permits, as a second choice, the spellings
     ACKNOWLEDGEMENT and JUDGEMENT.

15.   The following words are further examples of exceptions to the rule
that the final e̱ is retained before adding an ending that starts with a
consonant:

     argue, argument   nine, ninth
     true, truly   whole, wholly

In some of the examples above, retaining the e̱ would tend to produce an
additional syllable. (NINETH, TRUELY, and WHOLELY are incorrect
spellings, but NINETY is correct.)
     DUEL has two syllables, so DUELY would tend to be pronounced with

three syllables. The -ly form of DUE is actually _____.

_ _ _ _ _ _ _ _ _ _ _ _ _ _

     duly

16.   As you have seen, when the basic word ends in a consonant, you
merely add the ending to form a longer word. A notable exception is
the adjective form of WOOL. Does WOOLLY look peculiar to you? That
is the preferred spelling, although WOOLY is given as a second choice
in the dictionary. (The ending to form an adjective is -y, not -ly. The
ending -ly is used to form adverbs.)
     COOLLY follows the regular rule for adding an ending when the basic
word ends in a consonant. If you do not follow the rule in writing the
adverb form of COOL, you end up with COOLY, an unskilled laborer from
the Orient. Because of this confusion, the preferred spelling of the Asian
worker is now COOLIE.

The overseer, his _____ sheep dog at his
(adjective form of WOOL)

side, _____ observed the efforts of each
(adverb form of COOL)

_____ in his crew.
(unskilled Asian laborer)

- - - - - - - - - - - - - - -

woolly, coolly, coolie (or cooly)

17. Pay particular attention to words in which the <u>last</u> letter of the basic word is the same as the <u>first</u> letter of the ending. In such words,
there is a temptation to omit a letter, but be careful to preserve the
entire ending (-ness, -ly, -less, -like). Here are some examples of
such words:

cool	tail	jewel
coolly	tailless	jewellike

Many communities have harshly enforced laws against public

_____.
(-ness form of DRUNK)

- - - - - - - - - - - - - - -

drunkenness

18. The wise teacher looked at his students with an _____like
(like an OWL)

stare.

- - - - - - - - - - - - - -

owllike

19. Sometimes two endings are added to a basic word. DRUNKENNESS,
for example, is the basic word DRUNK, plus -en to form DRUNKEN, and
then -ness to form DRUNKENNESS.

How many endings are in the word CAREFULLY? _____

- - - - - - - - - - - - - -

two (The endings -ful and -ly are added to the basic word CARE.)

20. When some other ending is added to a word with an -ly ending to make a longer word, -ly becomes -li. You can see this change in words like FRIENDLINESS, LIKELIHOOD, and LIVELIER.

Circle the word that is correctly spelled:

> livelyhood   livelihood

– – – – – – – – – – – – – –

livelihood

Note: This tendency to change y to i in longer words is very common. The past tense of BURY is BURIED, and the plural of FERRY is FERRIES. The final y is discussed in detail in Chapter 5.

21. "Clean_____ is next to God_____" is a very old saying.

– – – – – – – – – – – – – –

Cleanliness, Godliness

22. Adding the ending -like to a basic word that ends in -ll can cause a problem. Avoid a triple l by using a hyphen, as in BELL-LIKE.

The hiker was guided by the _____ rise in the land
                                    (like a KNOLL)
before him.

– – – – – – – – – – – – – –

knoll-like

SELF-TEST

Circle each misspelled word below and write the correct spelling in the space beside it.

1.	arguement	_____	11. mileage	_____
2.	management	_____	12. truely	_____
3.	encloseure	_____	13. agreable	_____
4.	advisory	_____	14. dyeing	_____
5.	likelyhood	_____	15. wholy	_____
6.	development	_____	16. guidance	_____
7.	drunkeness	_____	17. healthfull	_____
8.	judgment	_____	18. pleasure	_____
9.	advantagous	_____	19. adventurous	_____
10.	plebian	_____	20. basic	_____

ANSWERS TO SELF-TEST

1. argument
3. enclosure
5. likelihood
7. drunkenness
9. advantageous

10. plebeian
12. truly
13. agreeable
15. wholly
17. healthful

CHAPTER 3
Double Trouble

Spelling would be a lot simpler if one always knew when to double (and when not to double) a final consonant before adding an ending to make a longer word. There are rules that generally make sense, there are exceptions to those rules, and there are apparent exceptions that are really rules for special cases.

Why does WRITE have one t while WRITTEN has two? Why is FILL-ING spelled with two l's while FILING is spelled with one? It depends on whether the vowel in the basic word (or word part) is long or short.

Consider the forms of WRITE, which so many people misspell. The base form, WRITE, follows the silent e rule. Since the word is pronounced with a long i, it ends with a silent e. Without the silent e, you have WRIT, which is a document or order from some court or official agency.

1. WRITING and WRITTEN illustrate the basic rule for deciding whether to double the consonant before the ending. Circle the word below that is pronounced with a long i:

     writing   written

- - - - - - - - - - - - - - -

   writing

2. The basic rule for doubling a final consonant is this: Double the final consonant if the preceding vowel is short, but do not double it if the vowel is long. (This rule applies only to words with a single vowel preceding a single final consonant. It does not apply to words like TREADING and SISTER.)

The -ing form of PLANE is _____.

- - - - - - - - - - - - - - -

   planing

3. The –ing form of PLAN is _____.

– – – – – – – – – – – – – –

  planning

4. There is a _____ a̱ in PLANING.
            (long/short)

– – – – – – – – – – – – – –

  long

5. The i̱ in FITTING is _____.
                    (ĭ/ī)

– – – – – – – – – – – – – –

  ĭ

6. The i̱ in DINING is _____.
                  (long/short)

– – – – – – – – – – – – – –

  long

7. If you did not double the ṉ in PLANNING, the short a̱ would become
a long a̱:

       plāne, plāning   plăn, plănning

If you did not double the ṯ in FITTING, you would end up with a word that
sounds like FIGHTING.
     Double the final consonant before adding the ending if the vowel before

the final consonant of the basic word is _____.
                                    (long/short)

– – – – – – – – – – – – –

  short

8. One who DINES is a _____, but the meal he eats in the

evening is _____.

– – – – – – – – – – – – – –

  diner, dinner

9. As you have seen, some of the endings that make longer words when added to a basic word part (sometimes doubling the final consonant) are –ing, –er, and –en. The following table shows more of these endings and relates the vowel sound to the single or doubled final consonant.

Long Vowels		Short Vowels	
Basic Word	Word + Ending	Basic Word	Word + Ending
fate	fated	fat	fatten
cane	caning	can	canning
			cannery
bite	biter	bit	bitten
			bitter
grime	grimy	grim	grimmer
wine	winery	win	winner
			winning
hope	hoping	hop	hopping
			hopper
tone	toner	ton*	tonnage*
cute	cutest	cut	cutting
			cutter
tune	tuned	stun	stunned
			stunning

*The sound of the o here is short u, which is true of many words with the –on combination.

Try completing a similar table with your own examples. Do not use s endings.

Long Vowels		Short Vowels	
Basic Word	Word + Ending	Basic Word	Word + Ending
_____	mated	mat	_____
	_____		_____
rope	roped	_____	dropped
	_____		_____
_____	riper	rip	_____
	_____		_____

- - - - - - - - - - - - - - -

Long Vowels		Short Vowels	
Basic Word	Word + Ending	Basic Word	Word + Ending
mate	mated mating	mat	matted matter matting
rope	roped roper roping	drop	dropped dropper dropping
ripe	ripen riper ripest	rip	ripped ripper

Note: You might have thought of other examples. If so, just compare with the examples given to be sure they follow the proper rules.

10. A beautiful double play was ruined when the second baseman

_____ the ball.

(past of DROP)

_ _ _ _ _ _ _ _ _ _ _ _ _

dropped

11. The restaurant was given a four–star _____.

(form of RATE)

_ _ _ _ _ _ _ _ _ _ _ _ _

rating

12. It should be clear by now that the final consonant of a one–syllable word is doubled before adding endings like -ing, -ed, and -er if the preceding vowel is <u>short</u>. If the vowel is <u>long</u>, the final consonant is <u>not</u> doubled. (Remember that we are talking about a single vowel preceding a single final consonant.)

The only common exception to this rule is BUS, which has the longer forms BUSES, BUSED, and BUSING. The plural of gas is GASES, but the longer forms, GASSED and GASSING, follow the rule.

The -ing form of BUS is _____. The -ing form of

GAS is _____.

_ _ _ _ _ _ _ _ _ _ _ _ _

busing, gassing

13. In dealing with longer words, you have two things to consider. As usual, decide whether the vowel preceding the final consonant is long or short. Then decide where the main accent is placed in the word.

The accent in COMPEL is on the second syllable, since that is the syllable that is pronounced more strongly:

com pel′

COMPEL is often misspelled (with a double l) because of this accent. This is also true of words like PROPEL, EXPEL, and REPEL.

The accent in PROFIT is on the first syllable:

pro′fit

Mark the accent in EXHIBIT:

ex hib it

_ _ _ _ _ _ _ _ _ _ _ _ _

ex hib it

14. The accent in OCCUR is on the _____ syllable.

(first/second)

– – – – – – – – – – – – – – –

    second (oc cur′)

15. Which syllable has the accent in BENEFIT? _____

– – – – – – – – – – – – – – –

    the first (ben′e fit)

16. Study the following words:

      compel, compelled, compelling
      occur, occurred, occurring, occurrence
      rebut, rebutted, rebutting

When the accent falls on the last syllable of a word, the final con-

sonant _____ doubled before adding the suffix.

      (is/is not)

– – – – – – – – – – – – – – –

  is

Note: The only common exception to this rule is CHAGRIN,
CHAGRINED.

17. After studying the market survey, the large dairies

_____ that many housewives _____ mar-
  (form of ADMIT)   (form of PREFER)
garine over butter because of its lower cost.

– – – – – – – – – – – – – – –

    admitted, preferred

18. Study the following words:

      benefit, benefited, benefiting
      differ, differed, differing, different
      focus, focused, focusing

When the accent does not fall on the last syllable of a word,

_____ the final consonant before adding the suffix.
  (double/do not double)

– – – – – – – – – – – – – – –

    do not double

19. The circus train derailed while _____ from Buffalo
                                    (form of TRAVEL)
to New York City.

— — — — — — — — — — — — — —

   traveling

20. The photographer had trouble _____ his camera.
                                  (form of FOCUS)

— — — — — — — — — — — — — —

   focusing

21. When the general manager was _____ , the company
                                 (form of EXPEL)

_____ by the new man's _____ approach.
(form of PROFIT)   (form of DIFFER)

— — — — — — — — — — — — — —

   expelled, profited, different (or differing)

22. The great earthquake and fire of 1906 was San Francisco's most
notable _____ .
        (occurence/occurrence)

— — — — — — — — — — — — — —

   occurrence

23. It is imp _____ to make water burn.

— — — — — — — — — — — — — —

   impossible

24. After _____ to several prior decisions, the
              (-ence form of REFER)

attorney _____ to the judgment of the court and
              (-ed form of DEFER)

_____ his appeal.
  (form of CANCEL)

— — — — — — — — — — — — — —

   reference, deferred, canceled

25. Some basic words have the accent on the last syllable, but the stress
is shifted in other forms of the words. Thus, they follow the rule:

      defer, deferred, deferring, but deference
      prefer, preferred, preferring, but preferable, preference

Longer forms of CANCEL follow the rule except for CANCELLATION.
Other exceptions are:

      crystal, crystallize
      question, questionable, but questionnaire

   The promoter announced _____ of the
                                (-tion form of CANCEL)

_____ medicine show before public opposition had a
  (-ing form of TRAVEL)

chance to _____.
              (-ize form of CRYSTAL)

— — — — — — — — — — — — — —

   cancellation, traveling, crystallize

26. The basic rules involving endings have now been discussed. There are a few more rules, but you can breathe easier now because there are virtually no more exceptions, and the rules themselves are very straight-forward.

Do <u>not</u> double the final consonant of the basic word when the word ends in more than one consonant:

> confirm, confirming, confirmation
> depend, dependable, depending, dependence *

We arrived at the theater ten minutes after the _____
(form of PERFORM)
had begun.

- - - - - - - - - - - - - - -

performance

27. Retain both consonants before adding the ending when a basic word ends with a double consonant:

> embarrass, embarrassing, embarrassment
> enroll, enrolling, enrollment

The young executive was infatuated with his secretary, but she tact-

fully _____ his attempts to date her.
  (form of REBUFF)

- - - - - - - - - - - - - - -

rebuffed

28. Do <u>not</u> double the final consonant of a basic word if the ending starts with a consonant:

> broad, broadcast
> develop, development

Succession to the throne required that the new king be a member of

the _____ ty and had nothing to do with his talent for
  (form of ROYAL)

_____ship.
  (form of LEAD)

- - - - - - - - - - - - - - -

royalty, leadership

_____

*Chapter 17 deals with words ending in -ance and -ence.

29. Do not double the final consonant of a basic word if it is preceded by more than one vowel:

> treat, treated, treating
> equal, equalize
> need, needy
> obtain, obtainable

The patient _____ to be making a
(-ed form of APPEAR)

_____ recovery.
(form of SPEED)

- - - - - - - - - - - - - -

appeared, speedy

SELF-TEST

1. Circle each word below that is misspelled and write the correct spelling in the space beside it.

(a) canery _____   (j) stopper _____

(b) dutiful _____   (k) buter _____

(c) rabbit _____   (l) droping _____

(d) occurence _____   (m) scatter _____

(e) better _____   (n) furious _____

(f) ploted _____   (o) funnel _____

(g) manner _____   (p) finnery _____

(h) driling _____   (q) settled _____

(i) droned _____   (r) chery _____

2. Write the required from of each of the following words.

(a) compel _____ing   (k) inhibit _____ing

(b) occur _____ence   (l) rebut _____ed

(c) bus _____ed   (m) omit _____ing

(d) chagrin _____ed   (n) prefer _____ence

(e) benefit _____ing   (o) focus _____ing

(f) differ _____ent   (p) question _____aire

(g) profit _____ing   (q) demand _____ing

(h) travel _____ed   (r) embarrass _____ment

(i) cancel _____tion   (s) develop _____ing

(j) gas _____ing   (t) commercial _____ize

ANSWERS TO SELF-TEST

1. (a) cannery
   (d) occurrence
   (f) plotted
   (h) drilling

   (k) butter
   (l) dropping
   (p) finery
   (r) cherry

2. (a) compelling
   (b) occurrence
   (c) bused
   (d) chagrined
   (e) benefiting
   (f) different
   (g) profiting
   (h) traveled
   (i) cancellation
   (j) gassing

   (k) inhibiting
   (l) rebutted
   (m) omitting
   (n) preference
   (o) focusing
   (p) questionnaire
   (q) demanding
   (r) embarrassment
   (s) developing
   (t) commercialize

CHAPTER 4

The Sounds of *C, G,* and *S*

As you have learned, the silent e has an effect on the preceding vowel; it also has an effect on some consonants. Three consonants (c, g, and s) have two different sounds each:

> c sounds like k or s
> g sounds like guh or j
> s sounds like s or z

These consonants are said to be either hard or soft. This chapter will teach you to apply these sound distinctions to some common spelling problems.

1. If you will study the two lists of sample words below, you will see how the e changes the sound of the preceding consonant. (Perhaps it is time to stop referring to the e as silent, since it often has a sound in longer words.)

Hard Consonant	Soft Consonant
rag	rage
cog	cogent
attic	suffice
sac*	ace
tic*	ice

When c has the sound of s, it is a _____ c.
(hard/soft)

- - - - - - - - - - - - - - -

soft

---

*SAC means a baglike part of a plant or animal, and TIC is a muscular twitch. When an ordinary bag is meant, we spell it SACK; when we refer to a parasite, the sound of a watch, or the outside of a mattress, we spell it TICK.

2. When g has the sound of guh, it is a _____ g.

(hard/soft)

- - - - - - - - - - - - - -

hard

3. When c has the sound of k, it _____ usually followed by e.

(is/is not)

- - - - - - - - - - - - - -

is not

4. One of these words includes a hard g. Circle it.

sag   sage

- - - - - - - - - - - - - -

sag

5. The hard and soft sounds of c and of g are easy to tell apart, but the distinction between hard and soft s is more subtle. A memory aid might help. Think of the hard s as strong and the soft s as weak. The poison of a hissing snake's bite is strong; that of a buzzing bee's sting is weak. Hard s sounds like the s in HISS. Soft s sounds like the z in BUZZ.

The first s in SURPRISE is _____.

(hard/soft)

- - - - - - - - - - - - - -

hard

6. The second s in SURPRISE sounds like _____.

(s/z)

- - - - - - - - - - - - - -

z

7. Look at this pair of words:

  advice   advise

If you ADVISE someone, you give ADVICE. When a noun is derived from a verb, the distinction is sometimes made by changing s to c.

  If you DEVISE something, you make a _____ .

- - - - - - - - - - - - -

  device

8. The c in DEVICE has the sound of a _____ s.
  <u>   </u>   (hard/soft)

- - - - - - - - - - - - - -

  hard

  Note: Soft c always sounds like hard s.

9. You can't always be sure that the s will change to c. Many words (for example, SURPRISE and SERVICE) have the same spellings for noun and verb forms. But if the end of a word has the sound of hard s, you can be sure that the ending is ce. If the final sound is soft s, the ending is usually se. It might be ze, but it will not be ce! (-Ize, -yze, and -ise endings are discussed in Chapter 14.)

  The c in PRACTICE sounds like _____ .
                                    (s/z)

- - - - - - - - - - - - - -

  s

10. Circle the correctly spelled word in each of the following pairs:

  despice   servise
  despise   service

- - - - - - - - - - - - - - -

  despise, service

11. Study the sounds of ce, ci, and cy in the following words:

tracer	facing	racy
services	criticism	cyst
introduce	producing	policy

The above examples show that c sounds like _____ when followed
                                              (s/k)
by e, i, or y.

_ _ _ _ _ _ _ _ _ _ _ _ _ _

   s

12. The -ing form of PRACTICE is _____.

_ _ _ _ _ _ _ _ _ _ _ _ _ _

   practicing

13. A word that means "having the flavor of SPICE" is _____y.

_ _ _ _ _ _ _ _ _ _ _ _ _

   spicy

14. The -ed form of INTRODUCE is _____.

_ _ _ _ _ _ _ _ _ _ _ _ _ _

   introduced

15. The -er form of ENTICE is _____.

_ _ _ _ _ _ _ _ _ _ _ _ _

   enticer

16. Do you have trouble deciding whether a word should end in cy or sy?
If so, you are not alone. Some words are not much of a problem because
there are related words that clearly have an s near the end:

     rose, rosy
     ease, easy
     jealous, jealousy

The trouble comes with longer words, and there are clues to help you in
only a few words. Study the following examples:

     autocrat, autocracy   immediate, immediacy

If the basic word ends in -at or -ate, the ending of the longer form is
-cy.

   A DEMOCRAT is one who believes in government by the people, or

a dem_____.

_ _ _ _ _ _ _ _ _ _ _ _ _ _

   democracy

17. Unfortunately, most longer words ending in cy or sy follow no set pattern. Here are some examples of each type:

cy	sy
bankruptcy	ecstasy
idiocy	heresy
normalcy	hypocrisy
policy	idiosyncrasy

If you are unsure of longer words, it's best to use your dictionary. Even if you have the ending right, you might make some other mistake. Could you spell IDIOSYNCRASY without the dictionary? (You might need the dictionary to find out what it means!)

The religious leader freely admitted his her_____, but he insisted that no one could accuse him of hypo_____.

- - - - - - - - - - - - - -

heresy, hypocrisy

18. The failing company had to declare bank_____.

- - - - - - - - - - - - - -

bankruptcy

19. Circle each word below that is misspelled and write the correct spelling in the space beside it.

(a) servicing _____   (f) hypocricy _____

(b) introdusing _____   (g) democrasy _____

(c) practiced _____   (h) bankruptsy _____

(d) policy _____   (i) attic _____

(e) exercice _____   (j) embraced _____

- - - - - - - - - - - - - -

(b) introducing; (e) exercise; (f) hypocrisy; (g) democracy; (h) bank-ruptcy

If you intend to rest pretty soon, this would be a good place.

20. One of these words includes a hard c̲. Circle it.

    service   racket

— — — — — — — — — — — — — —

    racket

21. If the k̲ were left out of RACKET, the c̲ would have the sound of

_____.
  (c/s)

— — — — — — — — — — — — — —

    s

    Note: The e̲ after c̲ almost always indicates that the c̲ has the sound
    of s̲.

22. The a̲ in RACK is _____.
                        (long/short)

— — — — — — — — — — — — — —

    short

23. The a̲ in RAKE is pronounced as _____.
                                    (ă/ā)

— — — — — — — — — — — — — —

    ā

24. The o̲ in SOCKET is pronounced as _____.
                                     (ŏ/ō)

— — — — — — — — — — — — — —

    ŏ

25. Perhaps you are beginning to see that the c̲k̲ combination is not just an example of overkill. The k̲ without the c̲ would tend to indicate that the preceding vowel has a long sound.* Actually, the vowel before c̲k̲ has a short sound. Always! A great many common words end in c̲k̲: TACK, PECK, STICK, SMOCK, TRUCK. The vowel is short in all of them.

Here are some sets of words. One word in each line is misspelled. Circle the misspelled words.

brake, braket, bracket

pike, picket, piket

poke, pocket, poket

— — — — — — — — — — — — — —

The misspelled words are braket, piket, and poket.

26. Here are more sets of words. Circle the one word in each line that is misspelled.

thick, thicket, thiket

dock, doket, docket

beck, beckon, becon

truck, truker, trucker

— — — — — — — — — — — — — —

The misspelled words are thiket, doket, becon, and truker.

27. These frames were designed to help you see that k̲e̲ follows a long vowel, while c̲k̲ follows a vowel with a short sound. However, this is true only in the case of s̲i̲n̲g̲l̲e̲ vowels. Compare BECKON and BEACON. Chapter 7 shows how combinations of two vowels are used to indicate long vowel sounds.

---

*The only common exception is TREK, TREKKED, TREKKING.

The sound of c̲ is always hard when it is the last letter of a word. Following the pattern of the examples shown below, complete the other words in each column. Use your dictionary if necessary.

tic	ice
aspic	spice
spas_ _ _	pr_ _ _
rus_ _ _	sl_ _ _
pan_ _	n_ _ _

- - - - - - - - - - - - -

spastic	price
rustic	slice
panic	nice

28. A great many words end in c̲, and the preceding vowel is usually i̲. Most such words have longer forms, but they are very regular. The endings all follow the pattern of MUSIC, MUSICAL, MUSICALLY. Use this pattern to fill in the indicated forms below:

music	musical	musically
automatic		_____
electric	_____	_____
economic	_____	_____
asthmatically		_____

- - - - - - - - - - - - -

	automatically
electrical	electrically
economical	economically
	asthmatically

29. The longer forms of a few words do cause some trouble. The main problem words are:

arc	garlic	picnic
colic	mimic	politic
frolic	panic	traffic

Now suppose you wanted to write another form of one of these words, such as PICNIC. If you just added the ending, as you do for the soft c words, here is what would happen: A person going on a picnic would be called a PICNICER (sounds like pick nicer), and the act of going on a picnic would be PICNICING. (Remember the rule that c followed by e, i, or y has the sound of s?) How do you preserve the sound of k? Almost always by adding a k after the c and then adding the ending.

Here are the ordinary forms of all nine problem words:

arc, arced, arcing*

colic, colicky

frolic, frolicker, frolicked, frolicking, frolicky, frolicsome

garlic, garlicky

mimic, mimicked, mimicking, mimicry

panic, panicked, panicking, panicky

picnic, picnicker, picnicked, picnicking

politic, politics, politicker, politicking

Note that three words in the above list (FROLICSOME, MIMICRY, and POLITICS) do not have a k in the longer form. In these cases, the c is followed by a consonant, and the hard sound is automatically preserved. The other words on the list have forms ending in s, but they are either plurals or singular verb forms. (POLITICS is not the plural of POLITIC.)

Now you try a few. The past tense of PANIC is _____.

- - - - - - - - - - - - - - - -

panicked

---

*The first word on the list is an exception! The dictionary does allow you to spell the other forms of ARC with ck (ARCKED, ARCKING), but you see that these spellings look peculiar. That's because they are rarely spelled that way.

30. Don't forget the pickles when the family goes p_____ing.

– – – – – – – – – – – – – –

    picnicking

31. The playful colt f_____ed in the meadow.

– – – – – – – – – – – – – –

    frolicked

32. The –ing form of ARC is _____.

– – – – – – – – – – – – – –

    arcing

    Note: If you wrote ARCKING, you are not wrong, but the preferable
    form is without the k.

33. Circle each word below that is misspelled and write the correct
spelling in the space beside it.

(a) trafficking _____   (g) garlic   _____

(b) mimickry   _____   (h) arced   _____

(c) political   _____   (i) mimicked   _____

(d) frolicky   _____   (j) colicy   _____

(e) picniced   _____   (k) frolicsome _____

(f) panicy   _____   (l) picnicker   _____

– – – – – – – – – – – – – –

    (b) mimicry; (e) picnicked; (f) panicky; (j) colicky

34. The difficulties with hard and soft c show up mostly at the ends of
words. The hard and soft g sounds, on the other hand, usually cause
trouble at the beginnings of words.
    The initial hard g is no problem. If the first sound in the spoken word
(or syllable) is guh, the word is spelled with a g. Examine this list of
sample words:

galley	goblet	gullible
gangster	gossip	gusset
cigar	cargo	argument

The sound of g in the combinations ga, go, and gu is always

_____.
(hard/soft)

- - - - - - - - - - - -

hard

Note: The only common exception to this rule is found in the word
MARGARINE, which is a form of the older word OLEOMARGARINE.
The g in this word sounds like j, although that was not always true.

35. Now look at the following words:

gift	giblet
gild	gigolo
gibbon	fragile

The combination gi usually has the sound of _____.

(g/j/?)

- - - - - - - - - - - -

? (The gi can be pronounced with a g or a j sound.)

36. Study the following sample words:

gypsy	gymnasium
gyroscope	gynecology

In words starting with gy, the sound of g is _____.

(hard/soft)

- - - - - - - - - - - -

soft

Note: Many people are beginning to pronounce GYNECOLOGY with a
first syllable that sounds like GUY, so this will probably become an
exception. However, there is no spelling problem because Webster's
New Collegiate Dictionary does not list a single English word beginning with jy!

37. The soft g causes far more problems than hard g. Study the following words:

general	cage
germinate	savage
gesture	stranger
gelatin	avenge

The sound of g in the combination ge is usually _____.

(guh/j)

- - - - - - - - - - - -

j

38. MacArthur, Eisenhower, and Black Jack Pershing were all famous

_____.

– – – – – – – – – – – – – –

generals

39. The Texas _____ were the most famous group of
lawmen in the Old West.

– – – – – – – – – – – – – –

Rangers

40. Circle the combination that is most likely to have the sound of j:

ga   ge   gi   go   gu

– – – – – – – – – – – – –

ge

41. Far more words begin with ge than with je. Probably the best way
to avoid misspelling ge words with a j is to look in the je section of your
dictionary, mentally noting those words you are likely to use.
      When you read through the je section of the dictionary, you will come
upon the word JERKIN, which is a kind of jacket. It happens that there is
is a kind of cucumber called a GHERKIN.

How is the sound of j avoided in GHERKIN? _____

– – – – – – – – – – – – – –

An h follows the g.

42. Only one other common word starts with ghe. Can you think of it?

_____

– – – – – – – – – – – – –

ghetto

43. A few words begin with gha or gho, although the sound of g would be
hard even without the h. The main basic words in this class are:

ghastly   ghost   ghoul

Horror stores are filled with _____ and
                                    (grave robbers)
_____ and _____ crimes.
(disembodied spirits)   (grisly)

---

ghouls, ghosts, ghastly

44. The more common way of preserving the hard g sound is by means of the combination gu preceding the vowels e or i. The main words in this category are:

Guernsey	guidance	guilt
guerrilla	guide	guinea
guess	guild	guise
guest	guile	guitar

The islands in the Channel Islands, Jersey and _____, are better known to Americans as breeds of cows.

Guernsey

45. The jury, noting that the thief seemed to be fond of stringed instruments, found him _____ of stealing two violins, a banjo, and a Spanish g_____.

---

guilty, guitar

46. The President of the Screen Actor's G_____ was the _____ of honor at a testimonial dinner.

Guild, guest

47. One more word deserves special consideration. Many people misspell GAUGE because they try to be logical. Almost always, au is pronounced "aw," although in a few words it is pronounced "oh." There is no logical way to pronounce GAUGE to rhyme with CAGE, so many people misspell it GUAGE. Somehow they know the word contains a u, and they try to put it where it makes the most sense. That problem will eventually disappear because the modern spelling, GAGE, is enjoying more frequent usage. If you prefer the conventional spelling, spell it GAUGE.

Circle each word below that is misspelled and write the correct spelling in the space beside it.

(a) gigolo _____ (h) goulish _____

(b) manajer _____ (i) guinea _____

(c) disguise _____ (j) gile _____

(d) gesture _____ (k) ghostly _____

(e) jypsy _____ (l) guidance _____

(f) jester _____ (m) gymnasium _____

(g) gilty _____ (n) revenge _____

- - - - - - - - - - - - - -

(b) manager; (e) gypsy; (g) guilty; (h) ghoulish; (j) guile

SELF-TEST

Circle each misspelled word below and write the correct spelling in the space beside it.

1.	mimicry	_____	13. democrasy	_____
2.	frolicing	_____	14. gymnastick	_____
3.	piket	_____	15. getto	_____
4.	gelatin	_____	16. policy	_____
5.	bankruptcy	_____	17. guage	_____
6.	marjarine	_____	18. ghastly	_____
7.	politicks	_____	19. stranjer	_____
8.	servising	_____	20. practiced	_____
9.	generous	_____	21. despise	_____
10.	Gernsey	_____	22. gost	_____
11.	Jersey	_____	23. hypocrisy	_____
12.	guidance	_____	24. guilt	_____

ANSWERS TO SELF-TEST

2.	frolicking	13.	democracy
3.	picket	14.	gymnastic
6.	margarine	15.	ghetto
7.	politics	17.	gauge (or gage)
8.	servicing	19.	stranger
10.	Guernsey	22.	ghost

Part Two

Part 1 presented the basic ground rules of spelling, all of them hinging on the distinction between long and short vowels. Part 2 includes chapters that each concentrate on a particular part of a word. The chapters do not depend on each other, so they can be read in any order. When you complete this part, you will be able to:

- correctly spell longer forms of words ending in y;

- apply the general rules for forming plurals;

- apply general guidelines for choosing the correct combination of letters to express a long vowel sound;

- apply general guidelines for choosing the correct ei or ie combination for a particular word;

- choose the correct combination of letters to express the sh sound;

- correctly spell possessives and contractions;

- recognize incorrect spelling and spell correctly words formed from a prefix plus a basic word.

None of the rules presented in this part are "hard and fast," so you will also learn to spell correctly many exceptions to the guidelines offered.

CHAPTER 5

Final *Y*: Easy as Pie

In Chapters 2 and 3 you worked with spelling problems that occur when you wish to add an ending to a basic word. Before adding the ending, it is often necessary to add a letter (COMPEL, COMPELLING), to drop a letter (ENCLOSE, ENCLOSURE), or to change a letter (LIKELY, LIKE-LIHOOD).

Many people have special problems making longer words from basic words ending in y. The whole subject can be handled with just two rules. One rule deals with cases where the final y is preceded by a consonant and the other with cases where the final y is preceded by a vowel.

1. The basic word FERRY has the longer forms FERRIED, FERRIES, and FERRYING. Since FERRY ends with y that is preceded by a conso-nant, it is an example of one of the two rules mentioned above.

When the basic word ends in a y preceded by a consonant, change the

_____ to _____ before adding any ending except an ending that

starts with _____.

_ _ _ _ _ _ _ _ _ _ _ _ _ _

y, i, i

2. In the case of the basic word FERRY, the y is changed to i before adding -ed or -es, but the y is kept before adding -ing. (If you changed the y to i before adding -ing, you would have FERRIING, which looks very strange!)

Now study the following examples:

    copy, copying, copied
    beauty, beautiful
    try, tried, trying

Following the pattern of the sample words, write the indicated forms of the words on the next page.

(a) accompany _____ed   (c) identify _____ing

(b) certify _____able   (d) lively _____er

− − − − − − − − − − − − − −

   (a) accompanied; (b) certifiable; (c) identifying; (d) livelier

3. The _____ army _____ the
        (form of VICTORY)   (form of OCCUPY)

conquered country for ten years, insisted upon strict _____
                                                        (form of COMPLY)

with all regulations, and forbade any citizen to travel without

_____ papers on his person.
   (form of IDENTIFY)

− − − − − − − − − − − − − −

   victorious, occupied, compliance, identification (or identifying)

4. Study the following examples:

      buy, buyer, buying
      employ, employer, employee (or employe)
      fray, frayed, fraying

When the basic word ends in y preceded by a vowel (as in ARRAY),

_____ the basic word before adding the suffix.
   (change/do not change)

− − − − − − − − − − − − − −

   do not change

5. Write the indicated forms of the following words:

(a) destroy _____ed

(b) disobey _____ing

(c) pray _____er

− − − − − − − − − − − − − −

   (a) destroyed; (b) disobeying; (c) prayer

   Note: The preferred noun form of GAY is GAIETY, although GAYETY
   is not wrong. The ending -ety is rare when the basic word ends in y,
   so don't worry about it.

   The rules about final y with an s ending are the same plural rules
that apply for any other ending. Plurals are covered in Chapter 6.

SELF-TEST

Write the indicated form of each of the following words.

1.	ally	_____ed	10.	employ	_____able
2.	hurry	_____ing	11.	buoy	_____ant
3.	rely	_____able	12.	happy	_____ness
4.	essay	_____ist	13.	wacky	_____est
5.	identify	_____able	14.	duty	_____ful
6.	prey	_____ing	15.	pay	_____ee
7.	verify	_____cation	16.	luxury	_____ous
8.	defray	_____ed	17.	buy	_____er
9.	shiny	_____er	18.	lively	_____est

ANSWERS TO SELF-TEST

1.	allied	10.	employable
2.	hurrying	11.	buoyant
3.	reliable	12.	happiness
4.	essayist	13.	wackiest
5.	identifiable	14.	dutiful
6.	preying	15.	payee
7.	verification	16.	luxurious
8.	defrayed	17.	buyer
9.	shinier	18.	liveliest

CHAPTER 6
The Not-So-Simple Plurals

At first glance, plurals seem easy enough—just add s. If only it were that simple! True, the great majority of plurals end in s, but even then you have a couple of problems. Do you add s only, es, or something else?

Luckily, plurals have some definite rules with few exceptions. We'll start with some examples of each of these rules and let you try to figure out the rules.

1. Here are some examples of the simplest rule:

bed	book	writer	poem	mishap
beds	books	writers	poems	mishaps

Following the pattern of these examples, write the plurals of the following words:

(a) food   _____

(b) worker   _____

(c) habit   _____

— — — — — — — — — — — —

    (a) foods; (b) workers; (c) habits

2. If a word ends with a single _____ , add only the
                                       (consonant/vowel)

letter _____ .

— — — — — — — — — — — —

    consonant, s

Note: An obvious exception to this rule is the case of any word ending in s.

3. Now look at these examples:

hall	burr	well	muff
halls	burrs	wells	muffs

Following the pattern of these examples, write the plurals of the following words:

(a) bell _____

(b) wall _____

(c) buff _____

— — — — — — — — — — — — — —

  (a) bells; (b) walls; (c) buffs

4. If a word ends with a _____ consonant, add only the
                          (single/double)

letter _____.

— — — — — — — — — — — — — —

  double, s

5. Go through the alphabet mentally and try to think of a double consonant that does <u>not</u> follow this rule. What letter did you think of?

_____

— — — — — — — — — — — — — —

  s (Double <u>s</u> does not follow the rule, because you would then have a word ending in triple <u>s</u>! This does not happen in English, and probably not in any other language.)

6. For words ending in double <u>s</u>, form the plural by adding –es. Write the plurals of the following words:

(a) pass _____   (c) truss _____

(b) mess _____   (d) gloss _____

— — — — — — — — — — — — —

  (a) passes; (b) messes; (c) trusses; (d) glosses

7. A great many words end in a three-letter combination that includes a vowel and two <u>different</u> consonants. Here are a few examples:

farm	help	fist	fort	quirk
farms	helps	fists	forts	quirks

Following the pattern of these examples, write the plurals of the following words:

(a) burn   _____

(b) fault   _____

(c) mast   _____

- - - - - - - - - - - - - -

     (a) burns; (b) faults; (c) masts

8. Words ending in -ch and -sh are exceptions to the rule illustrated in frame 7. With these endings, the plural is always formed by adding -es. Here are some sample words with these endings:

catch	touch	mesh	brush	branch
catches	touches	meshes	brushes	branches

     Write the plurals of the following words:

(a) stretch _____   (d) crutch _____

(b) crash _____   (e) rush _____

(c) stench _____   (f) pinch _____

- - - - - - - - - - - - - -

     (a) stretches; (b) crashes; (c) stenches; (d) crutches; (e) rushes; (f) pinches

Note: Many of the words we have dealt with so far are verbs as well as nouns, but this makes no difference in the endings. Consider two sentences that include a form of the word STRETCH:

     Exercise stretches the muscles.
     The journey was marked by lovely stretches of scenery.

In the first sentence, STRETCHES is a verb; in the second, a noun. This chapter is about plurals, and only nouns have plurals, but remember that the word—and how it is spelled—is the same, regardless of the part of speech.

9. Look at the following words and their plurals:

maze   scene   sprite   rose   rule
mazes   scenes   sprites   roses   rules

Each of these words already ends in e, so the plural is formed by adding s. What could be simpler?
     Following the pattern of the examples above, write the plurals of the following words:

(a) Mennonite _____   (c) ferrule _____

(b) reprobate _____   (d) keynote _____

– – – – – – – – – – – – – – –

     (a) Mennonites; (b) reprobates; (c) ferrules; (d) keynotes

10. Earlier in the chapter, we developed this rule: If a word ends with a single consonant, add only s to form the plural. But look at these words and their plurals:

tax   box   fix   flux   hex
taxes   boxes   fixes   fluxes   hexes

We have an exception to the rule because words ending in x form the plural by adding -es.
     Write the plurals of the following words:

(a) ax   _____

(b) mix _____

(c) flex _____

– – – – – – – – – – – – – – –

     (a) axes; (b) mixes; (c) flexes

11. The plural of BUS deserves special mention. Following the silent e rule from Chapter 2, you would expect the plural of BUS to be BUSSES because of the short u. Not doubling the s (BUSES) would indicate a long u, as in FUSES and RUSES. However, such is not the case. Spelling changes with usage, and modern usage indicates a preference for the undoubled consonant when a word in the singular ends with a short vowel and a single s. If it is any consolation, the only two common words that show this peculiarity in the plural are BUS and GAS.

          The preferred forms of BUS are: BUSES, BUSED, BUSING.
          The preferred forms of GAS are: GASES, GASSED, GASSING.

There are a number of words of more than one syllable that end in us and in which the vowel is short. Some of these are:

focus	rebus	sinus
focuses	rebuses	sinuses

Each of these words has a final syllable that is _____.

(stressed/unstressed)

_ _ _ _ _ _ _ _ _ _ _ _ _ _ _

unstressed

12. Using the sample words in frame 11 as a guide, write the plural of RADIUS. _____

_ _ _ _ _ _ _ _ _ _ _ _ _ _ _

radiuses

Note: Latin students and super-spellers will know that RADII is an alternate plural for RADIUS, but right now we're concerned with -uses endings. In all words with similar endings, the plural is formed exactly as in the examples. Sometimes you have the option of using the Latin plural (FOCI, RADII), but you are safe if you follow the illustrated form.

13. Examine the following words and their plurals:

army	baby	rally	jetty	penny
armies	babies	rallies	jetties	pennies

Compare the words above with the following words:

bay	valley	monkey	buoy
bays	valleys	monkeys	buoys

Now try to figure out the rules for forming the plurals of words ending in y and apply them in the next few frames.

If a word ends in y preceded by a consonant, change the _____ to _____ and add _____.

_ _ _ _ _ _ _ _ _ _ _ _ _ _

y, i, es

14. If a word ends in y preceded by a vowel, add _____.

_ _ _ _ _ _ _ _ _ _ _ _ _ _

es

15. The plural of FERRY is _____.

- - - - - - - - - - - - -

    ferries

16. The plural of TURKEY is _____.

- - - - - - - - - - - - -

    turkeys

17. Let's summarize the general rules for forming plurals:

- If a word ends with a single consonant (except s or x), add s.
- If a word ends with a combination of consonants (except -ch and -sh), add s.
- If a word ends with -ch or -sh, add es.
- If a word ends in e, add s.
- If a word ends in x, add es.
- If a word ends in us, and the final syllable is unstressed, add es.
- If a word ends in y preceded by a consonant, change the y to i and add es.
- If a word ends in y preceded by a vowel, add s.

    Now try applying these rules. Write the plural of each of the following words:

(a) printer	_____	(g) reform	_____
(b) church	_____	(h) whippoorwill	_____
(c) crush	_____	(i) savage	_____
(d) isthmus	_____	(j) lottery	_____
(e) volley	_____	(k) ax	_____
(f) bus	_____	(l) gas	_____

- - - - - - - - - - - - -

    (a) printers; (b) churches; (c) crushes; (d) isthmuses; (e) volleys; (f) buses; (g) reforms; (h) whippoorwills; (i) savages; (j) lotteries; (k) axes; (l) gases

Note: A less familiar but also correct plural of ISTHMUS is ISTHMI. BUSES and GASES were noted earlier as exceptions.

If you need a break, this is a good place to stop.

18. Now let's consider some special cases. Look at these examples:

hero	Negro	domino
heroes	Negroes	dominoes

And these:

banjo	albino	piano
banjos	albinos	pianos

What you probably discovered from the foregoing examples is that when a word ends with o, there is no good rule for deciding whether to add s or es. True. On page 60 is a list of the commonly used words ending with o. The left column shows the words with the s ending, the right, words with the es ending. Only the plurals are shown.

o + s	o + es
albinos	bravoes
banjos	buffaloes
boleros	dominoes
burros	echoes
cameos	fiascoes
casinos	frescoes
cellos	heroes
concertos	innuendoes
crescendos	mosquitoes
dittos	mottoes
embryos	Negroes
folios	potatoes
ghettos	tomatoes
gigolos	tornadoes
halos	
kimonos	
mementos	
palominos	
patios	
photos	
pianos	
piccolos	
pimentos	
pimientos	
pistachios	
portfolios	
provisos	
rodeos	
scenarios	
silos	
sombreros	
stereos	
studios	
torsos	
zeros	

If you are discouraged by the lack of rhyme or reason in the foregoing plurals, take heart. The list shows the <u>preferred</u> spelling of each word, but the dictionary does show the alternate spelling as a second choice for a great many of the words. If you write ZEROES instead of ZEROS, for example, no one will know whether you picked the secondary spelling by accident or by choice.

Of course, you will usually want to use the preferred spelling, so here are some guidelines. If the word is very common in English, (ECHO, HERO, and POTATO, but not PIANO and ZERO), the ending is very likely to be es. If the word has been adopted without change from the Spanish, the ending is s only. As foreign words (usually Italian, Spanish, or Greek) come to look more like ordinary English words, the plural form gradually becomes es. In some circles, the Italian plural of certain words is used (CELLI, CONCERTI), but the English form is always correct.

A few English words end in oo, and in these cases the plural is no problem at all. It is rare in English to find three vowels together in a row, so the ending is s.

bamboos	igloos	shampoos
boos	kangeroos	tattoos
hullabaloos		

Write the preferred plural of each of the following words:

(a) albino _____   (i) potato _____

(b) buffalo _____   (j) proviso _____

(c) casino _____   (k) rodeo _____

(d) concerto _____   (l) silo _____

(e) domino _____   (m) sombrero _____

(f) ghetto _____   (n) tornado _____

(g) mosquito _____   (o) torso _____

(h) piano _____   (p) zero _____

- - - - - - - - - - - - - -

(a) albinos; (b) buffaloes; (c) casinos; (d) concertos; (e) dominoes; (f) ghettos; (g) mosquitoes; (h) pianos; (i) potatoes; (j) provisos; (k) rodeos; (l) silos; (m) sombreros; (n) tornadoes; (o) torsos; (p) zeros

19. Here are some words, singular and plural, whose orgins go all the way back to Greek:

Singular	Plural
analysis	analyses
basis	bases
crisis	crises
diagnosis	diagnoses

All such words ending in <u>is</u> form the plural by changing <u>is</u> to <u>es</u>.
    Write the plurals of the following words:

(a) axis   _____   (c) psychosis   _____

(b) neurosis _____   (d) thesis   _____

— — — — — — — — — — — — — —

    (a) axes; (b) neuroses; (c) psychoses; (d) theses

    Note: The plural of AX is also AXES, but that is just one of those coincidences so common in English.

20. Another group of Greek words causes trouble for two reasons. First, the singular and plural are quite different forms of the word; and second, people tend to use the plural form when the singular is intended. Here are some of the main words in this group:

Singular	Plural
criterion	criteria
ganglion	ganglia
phenomenon	phenomena

    It is hard to determine the most important single

_____ for selecting a winning candidate.
    (criterion/criteria)

— — — — — — — — — — — — —

    criterion

21. Nuclear physics is a field rich in striking scientific phen_____.

— — — — — — — — — — — — —

    phenomena

22. A fairly large number of Latin words also change the form for the plural. Typical of this group are the following:

Singular	Plural
compendium	compendia
datum	data
memorandum	memoranda
stadium	stadia

Some of the above words now have an English plural that is coming to be preferred: COMPENDIUMS, MEMORANDUMS, STADIUMS. But DATUM is rarely used; DATA is often used for both singular and plural, especially in computer work.

Insert the appropriate forms of the words (DATA, MEMORANDUM, STADIUM) in the following sentence:

According to the latest in a long series of _____,

all engineering _____ on the seven largest coliseum-

type _____ must be fed into the computer by June 30.

- - - - - - - - - - - - - - -

Preferred: memorandums, data, stadiums
Also correct: memoranda, data, stadia

23. One more important group of words from the Latin all end in x in the singular. Time has eroded the problem with these plurals because the -ces plural (standard not so many years ago) is gradually being replaced with the -es form. Either form is acceptable, but note that if you are using APPENDIX to mean a supplement at the back of the book, the only correct plural is APPENDIXES. Here are the principal words in this group with both the new and old plurals:

Singular	New Plural	Old Plural
apex	apexes	apices
appendix	appendixes	appendices
helix	helixes	helices
index	indexes	indices
matrix	matrixes	matrices

The compendium of meteorological phenomena included a detailed

i_____ and three a_____.

- - - - - - - - - - - - - - -

    index, appendixes

24. Even a few Hebrew words (CHERUB, SERAPH) have found their way into the English language with their Hebrew plurals (CHERUBIM, SERAPHIM) intact. Note, however, that when CHERUB is used to mean a small child rather than an angel, the correct plural is CHERUBS.
    Write the correct plurals of CHERUB in the following sentence:

> The little _____ at the birthday party were
>
> not at all like the _____ at St. Peter's
> Cathedral.

- - - - - - - - - - - - - - -

    cherubs, cherubim

25. Many ordinary English words have a different form for the plural, but they are so common as to present little difficulty in spelling:

foot	mouse	tooth	woman	child	ox
feet	mice	teeth	women	children	oxen

A few words, such as SHEEP and DEER, have the same form for singular and plural. They, too, are common enough to be no real spelling problem.
    Another word in this category deserves special consideration. Almost everyone is familiar with the "rolling bones" or "galloping dominoes" of gambling: a pair of DICE. Just one of these fickle cubes is properly called a DIE. However, a DIE is also any one of a number of machinist's tools, and the plural of the word, when used in this sense, is DIES.
    Insert the correct plurals of DIE:

> Cubes used in gambling are _____, while machin-
>
> ist's tools of certain types are called _____.

- - - - - - - - - - - - - - -

    dice, dies

26. Most words ending in f and all words ending in ff form the plural by adding s. Some of these are:

belief	chief	rebuff	skiff	tariff
beliefs	chiefs	rebuffs	skiffs	tariffs

However, many frequently used words ending in a single f form the plural by changing f to v and adding es:

half	leaf	self	shelf	thief
halves	leaves	selves	shelves	thieves

For the plural of words ending in fe, change the f to v and add es:

knife	life	wife
knives	lives	wives

If you are troubled by the absence of a definite rule that tells you when you should change a final f to v and add es, pronunciation will help you where exact rules don't. If there is a v in the plural, you can hear it in the spoken word. The sound of the spoken word also helps you in the case of CHAFES, which is another form (although not a plural) of CHAFE. You can hear the f! You can also hear the f in GIRAFFES, another exception.

Write the plural of the following words:

(a) belief _____   (f) calf _____

(b) mastiff _____   (g) sheaf _____

(c) rebuff _____   (h) myself   our_____

(d) handcuff _____   (i) brief _____

(e) tariff _____   (j) wife _____

- - - - - - - - - - - - - - -

(a) beliefs; (b) mastiffs; (c) rebuffs; (d) handcuffs; (e) tariffs;
(f) calves; (g) sheaves; (h) ourselves; (i) briefs; (j) wives

27. In a compound word (whether hyphenated or not), only the main element takes a plural form.

lieutenant general   mother-in-law

lieutenants general   mothers-in-law

Insert the appropriate forms of NOTARY PUBLIC and COURT-MARTIAL in the following sentence:

Six _____ provided affidavits to be sub-

mitted in the series of _____ of the seven accused soldiers.

- - - - - - - - - - - - - -

notaries public, courts-martial

28. The plural of abbreviations, letters, and numbers are formed by adding '<u>s</u>:

Ph.D.'s   Y.M.C.A.'s   e's   2's

MISSISSIPPI is spelled with four _____ and four _____.

- - - - - - - - - - - - - -

<u>i</u>'s, <u>s</u>'s

29. Registered nurses are often referred to as _____.

(abbreviation)

- - - - - - - - - - - - - -

R.N.'s

SELF–TEST

Write the plurals of the following words:

1.	editor	_____	18. bus	_____
2.	whippoorwill	_____	19. focus	_____
3.	address	_____	20. cranny	_____
4.	retort	_____	21. volley	_____
5.	bench	_____	22. canary	_____
6.	sandwich	_____	23. piano	_____
7.	smash	_____	24. zero	_____
8.	isotope	_____	25. motto	_____
9.	crux	_____	26. potato	_____
10.	kangeroo	_____	27. analysis	_____
11.	criterion	_____	28. memorandum	_____
12.	helix	_____	29. seraph	_____
13.	tariff	_____	30. shelf	_____
14.	knife	_____	31. giraffe	_____
15.	sister-in-law	_____	32. Y.W.C.A.	_____
16.	notary public	_____	33. M.D.	_____
17.	7	_____	34. z	_____

ANSWERS TO SELF-TEST

1. editors
2. whippoorwills
3. addresses
4. retorts
5. benches
6. sandwiches
7. smashes
8. isotopes
9. cruxes
10. kangeroos
11. criteria
12. helixes (or helices)
13. tariffs
14. knives
15. sisters-in-law
16. notaries public
17. 7's

18. buses
19. focuses
20. crannies
21. volleys
22. canaries
23. pianos
24. zeros
25. mottoes
26. potatoes
27. analyses
28. memorandums (or memoranda)
29. seraphim
30. shelves
31. giraffes
32. Y.W.C.A.'s
33. M.D.'s
34. z's

CHAPTER 7

The Long Vowel Sounds

The silent e is a common device to indicate the long sound of the preceding vowel, as in MATE, METE, BITE, CONE, and TUNE. It is by no
means the only way to indicate the long vowel sounds. At least forty-six
different combinations of two (and occasionally three) vowels are used in
English to represent the long sounds of a, e, i, o, and u. As you know,
w and y are sometimes vowels, although these letters are more often
seen as consonants. (For example, w is a vowel only in combination with
another vowel, as in AWL and HOWL.) Thus, many of the vowel combinations illustrated in this chapter include w or y.

The purpose of this chapter is to give you practice in recognizing the
use of vowel combinations to indicate long sounds. While there are no
rigid rules to go by, you will at least learn to pause before writing a
word of uncertain spelling, reviewing alternate ways of indicating the
long vowel sounds. Bear in mind that vowel combinations also indicate
other sounds (SOUND is an example), but this chapter deals only with the
long vowel sounds. Some combinations of vowels to produce long vowel
sounds are rare or at least unusual (including eo, oe, ae, uy, oi, eau,
au, oo, eu, ieu). Certain other combinations are common for indicating
one sound, but rare for showing another sound. Later in the chapter,
the common combinations will be separated from the rare ones.

1. The following words illustrate the vowel combinations used to indicate
the sound of long a (ā):

      rain   pay   break   veil   obey

The word pronounced māt is spelled MATE. (In this case the silent
e indicates a long a.) Write the words, written with two vowels together,
that correspond to the following pronunciations:

(a) stāk _____   (d) brā _____

(b) vān _____   (e) strān _____

(c) whā _____

-- -- -- -- -- -- -- -- -- -- -- --

(a) steak; (b) vain or vein; (c) whey; (d) bray; (e) strain

Note: STAKE and VANE are proper words, but they are not correct in this frame because they are not spelled with two vowels together.

2. The following words illustrate the vowel combinations used to indicate the sound of long e (ē). The words in the right column indicate examples of less common combinations.

feet	people
beam	Caesar
receive	quay*
key	Phoebe
field	

The word pronounced pēt is spelled PETE (again following the silent e rule). Write the words, written with two vowels together, that correspond to the following pronunciations:

(a) crēm _____

(b) bēt _____

(c) dē sēv _____

(d) kē _____

(e) yēld _____

-- -- -- -- -- -- -- -- -- -- -- --

(a) cream; (b) beat or beet; (c) deceive; (d) key or quay; (e) yield

Note: The combinations ei and ie are discussed further in Chapter 8.

3. Julius _____ , returning victorious from war, was extremely popular with the p_____ of Rome.

-- -- -- -- -- -- -- -- -- -- -- --

Caesar, people

_____

*Most people probably pronounce this word "kway," to rhyme with day. In any case, it is a very rare combination for the sound of long e.

4. The following words illustrate the vowel combinations used to indicate the sound of long i (ī). The words in the right column indicate examples of less common combinations.

die	eye
dye	aisle
height	aye
sky	buy
	choir

The word pronounced bīt is spelled BITE. Write the words, written with two vowels together, that correspond to the following pronunciations:

(a) rī _____   (c) bī _____

(b) hīt _____   (d) vī _____

- - - - - - - - - - - - - -

(a) rye; (b) height; (c) buy; (d) vie

Note: If you wrote WRY instead of RYE, remember that we were looking for two vowels together.

5. They had two good seats on the _____sle for the concert of the

Mormon Tabernacle _____.

- - - - - - - - - - - - - -

aisle, Choir

6. The following words illustrate the vowel combinations used to indicate the sound of long o (ō). The words in the right column indicate examples of less common combinations.

roam	sew
foe	yeoman
boulder	beau
row	hautboy
owe	brooch

The word pronounced kōr is spelled CORE. Write the words, written with two or more vowels together, that correspond to the following pronunciations:

(a) kōt _____   (d) stō _____

(b) shōl der _____   (e) tō _____

(c) ō _____

- - - - - - - - - - - - - - -

    (a) coat; (b) shoulder; (c) owe; (d) stow; (e) toe or tow

7. Circle the word below that has the sound of long o:

    pew   stew   sew   few

- - - - - - - - - - - - - -

    sew

8. The following words illustrate the vowel combinations used to indicate the sound of long u (ū). The words in the right column indicate examples of less common combinations.

few	beauty
view	feud
cue	queue
suit	lieu
you	

    The word pronounced tūn is spelled TUNE. Write the words, written with two or more vowels together, that correspond to the following pronunciations:

(a) stū _____

(b) rē vū _____

(c) sūt _____

(d) dū _____

- - - - - - - - - - - - - -

    (a) stew; (b) review; (c) suit; (d) due or dew

9. There is another sound of u that is almost long u. This sound occurs in words like FOOD and MOON. Many words with this sound are spelled with the same vowel combinations as long u. They include such words as CREW and UNCOUTH. (In the phonetic spelling, ū is used, but it is not quite right.)

    Love of money may be the _____ of all evil, but Sinatra, Como,
                          (rūt)

and others made a pile of it while _____ love ballads to suit
                                (krūn ing)

the _____ of the era. Meeting the needs of _____ is good busi-
      (mūd)   (yūth)

ness.

- - - - - - - - - - - - - -

    root, crooning, mood, youth

10. Circle each word below that is misspelled and correct the spelling:

At a point where the ralerode rounded a hill, blocking the

vue from the highway, the frate trane collided with a car

loded with tenagers on their way home from the beech.

— — — — — — — — — — — — — — —

railroad, view, freight, train, loaded, teenagers, beach

SELF–TEST

1. All the following words are misspelled. Correct the spellings.

(a) strane _____

(b) obay _____

(c) perceve _____

(d) Ceasar _____

(e) hight _____

(f) sprie _____

(g) approch _____

(h) althoe _____

(i) fude _____

(j) qeue _____

(k) buty _____

(l) fue _____

2. VANE and VEIN sound exactly alike, but they have different spellings because they have different meanings. Such words are called <u>homonyms</u>. Write a homonym for each of the following words:

(a) rain _____

(b) brake _____

(c) seize _____

(d) seem _____

(e) so _____

(f) throes _____

(g) hue _____

(h) cue _____

ANSWERS TO SELF–TEST

1. (a) strain

    (b) obey

    (c) perceive

    (d) Caesar

    (e) height

    (f) spry

    (g) approach

    (h) although

    (i) feud

    (j) queue

    (k) beauty

    (l) few

2. (a) rein or reign

    (b) break

    (c) cease or seas

    (d) seam

    (e) sew or sow

    (f) throws

    (g) hew or Hugh

    (h) queue

CHAPTER 8

"Except After *C*"

Chapter 7 was devoted to the many different ways the long vowel sounds are reproduced in writing by various combinations of vowels. Probably no other combination of vowels produces such torment in the minds of poor (and even good) spellers as ie and ei. The language is filled with these combinations and the writer is forever trying to decide which comes first—e or i.

No other spelling rule is so well known as that set forth in the following jingle:

> I before e
>   Except after c
> Or when sounded as a
>   As in NEIGHBOR and WEIGH.

Unfortunately, there are too many exceptions for that rule to be of much use. Better, but still not good enough, is:

> I before e when sounded as ee
>   (Except after c)
> Or when sounded as a
>   As in NEIGHBOR and WEIGH.

Some people memorize an additional sentence to illustrate some of the exceptions: NEITHER had LEISURE to SEIZE the WEIRD thing.

1. It is helpful to break down the ei and ie combinations into a few lists of examples. The longest list (and it is not all-inclusive) gives examples of ie pronounced as ee:

achieve	fiend	reprieve
apiece	fierce	shield
belief	frieze	shriek
believe	grief	siege
bier	niece	thief
brief	piece	tier
cashier	pier	wield
chief	pierce	yield
field	relieve	

In some cases the ie is softened somewhat when the next letter is r (as in CASHIER and FIERCE), but it's close enough. One very common ie word, often misspelled, is FRIEND. It doesn't belong in the above list because the ie pronunciation is too far away from ee, but it should be noted.

Circle the words in the following sentence that are misspelled and correct the spelling:

The feindish thief was relieved to find that his breif entries

into three separate offices on the pier yeilded more than

$500 apeice, but as the shrieks of the casheir in the third

office pierced the night, he fled straight into the arms of

an officer wielding a loaded revolver.

— — — — — — — — — — — — —

fiendish, brief, yielded, apiece, cashier

2. In almost all cases, after c the combination is ei. (The single exception to all ei rules is FINANCIER.)

ceiling	deceive
conceit	perceive
conceive	receipt*
deceit	receive

Circle the words in the following sentence that are misspelled and correct the spelling:

It is the height of conciet for a shopkeeper to try to decieve

a customer who holds a signed receipt for his money.

---

*Note the silent p.

- - - - - - - - - - - - -

    conceit, deceive

3. The following list includes most of the words in which the sound is
long <u>a</u> (more or less) and the combination is <u>ei</u>:

deign	heir	skein
eight	inveigh	sleigh
eighth	inveigle*	weigh
feign	neigh	weight
feint	reign	veil
freight	rein	vein
heinous		

Circle the words in the following sentence that are misspelled and
correct the spelling:

    The eighth riegning ruler of the small state deigned to

    weigh the charges only after the skiens of evidence in

    the hienous crime led directly to his hier.

- - - - - - - - - - - - -

    reigning, skeins, heinous, heir

4. When the sound is long <u>i</u>, the combination is <u>ei</u>, as in the following
words:

eider	kaleidoscope	sleight
height	seismograph	stein

Here is a list of words in which the sound is <u>ee</u> but the combination is
<u>ei</u>:

either	seize	weir
leisure	sheik	weird
neither		

---

*This word is also pronounced ĭn vē gle.

After the sound of <u>sh</u>, even though it follows <u>c</u>, the combination is <u>ie</u>, as in the following words:

ancient	omniscient	quotient
deficient	patient	species
efficient	proficient	transient

Circle the misspelled words in the following sentences and correct the spelling:

The Masquerade Ball was a wierd kaleidoscope of cos-

tumes and characters. The Anceint Mariner seized a

stien of beer to toast the Shiek of Araby, while Black-

stone the Magician, niether sober nor proficient, attract-

ed the leisurely interest of Lady Macbeth with some

slight of hand.

— — — — — — — — — — — — — —

weird, Ancient, stein, Sheik, neither, sleight

5. So far, all the combinations of <u>ie</u> and <u>ei</u> have been <u>diagraphs</u>. (A diagraph is a combination of two letters to produce a single sound.) But in many words each of the two vowels stands for a separate sound. These combinations are <u>not</u> diagraphs and therefore do not belong in any of the categories discussed so far in this chapter. In one such word, DEITY, <u>e</u> comes before <u>i</u>. Luckily, all the others are spelled with <u>ie</u>. A few of these words, divided into syllables, are shown below:

a′li en	me di e′val
au′di ence	no to ri′e ty
cloth′i er	qui′et
fi′er y	sci′ence
gai′e ty	so bri′e ty
gla′ci er	so ci′e ty
hi′er arch y	va ri′e ty

Circle the misspelled words in the following sentence and correct the spelling:

The firey sacrifice, by which many an ancient soceity ap-

peased a variety of local dieties, is alien to modern ex-

pereince.

— — — — — — — — — — — — — —

fiery, society, deities, experience

SELF-TEST

Circle each misspelled word and write the correct spelling in the space beside it.

1.	ceiling _____	11.	medeval _____
2.	recieve _____	12.	seismograph_____
3.	sleigh _____	13.	conciet _____
4.	achieve _____	14.	skien _____
5.	beleif _____	15.	seize _____
6.	feind _____	16.	niether _____
7.	sheild _____	17.	ancient _____
8.	wierd _____	18.	species _____
9.	friend _____	19.	alein _____
10.	thief _____	20.	gaiety _____

ANSWERS TO SELF-TEST

2.	receive	11.	medieval
5.	belief	13.	conceit
6.	fiend	14.	skein
7.	shield	16.	neither
8.	weird	19.	alein

CHAPTER 9

Sh-h-h!

Much emphasis in this book has been placed on beginnings and endings of words because one of the best ways to improve your spelling is to pay attention to these parts of words. There is plenty of room for error in the middle part of the word, too. But, it is very difficult to cover "mid-word" problems; the seemingly endless variety of such problems might easily overwhelm the student.

As you might guess from the title, this chapter will deal with one group of problems in the hearts of words—the sound of sh (that is, the other combinations of letters that sound like sh when the word is spoken).

1. Examine the following words, along with **the** letters that indicate the sound of sh in each:

ce	ocean	se	nauseous
ch	machine	si	expansion
ci	social	ss	tissue
s	erasure	ssi	impression
sci	conscious	ti	patient

If you remember that CRUSTACEANS such as lobsters live in the OCEAN and that young women are often CURVACEOUS, you have almost eliminated the problem of ce words. The others, such as HERBACEOUS plants and SEBACEOUS glands, are not very common.

A good figure was not her strong point; in fact, she was about as

_____ as a cr_____.

  (having CURVES)   (horny-shelled sea animal)

– – – – – – – – – – – –

  curvaceous, crustacean

2. The combination <u>ch</u> is found in the middle of only a few common words (MACHINE is the most common).* It is more likely to occur as the initial sound, and even these words are mostly French (see Supplement 4). The fairly common main words starting with <u>ch</u> are listed below:

chagrin	chaperon	chenille
chaise	charade	cheroot
chalet	chartreuse	chevron
chamois	chassis	chic
champagne	chateau	chicanery
chancre	chauffeur	chiffon
chandelier	chauvinism	chignon
chaparral	chef	chivalry
chapeau	chemise	

Fill in the blanks with appropriate words from the above list:

"I approve of many of the goals of the Women's Liberation

Movement," he said with some _____, "but the

normal inclination of a gentleman to act with _____

toward a female companion is somewhat crippled by the

charge of male _____."

– – – – – – – – – – – – – – –

chagrin, chivalry, chauvinism

*Here we are talking about <u>ch</u> with the sound of <u>sh</u>; <u>ch</u> in the written word has a number of difficult sounds, only one of which is <u>sh</u>.

3. The ci combination is found in a great many words. Often you have a clue that the sh sound is written ci if you can think of another form of the word that has c in about the same location, as illustrated by the words in parentheses in the list below. Sometimes, of course, such a clue does not exist, or it might exist in one related word but not another. Here are some of the words in this group:

crucial   species, special (specific)
facial (face)   sufficient (suffice)
glacial (glacier)   deficient
social (society)   efficiency

One of the crucial _____ problems of our time is that
                         (of SOCIETY)

of _____ tension, esp_____ in areas where there
      (of RACE)   (particularly)

are insuff_____ channels of communication between ethnic
              (inadequate)
groups with different cultural values.

– – – – – – – – – – – – – –

social, racial, especially, insufficient

4. The letter s alone often has the sound of sh when it is followed by u, as in ERASURE, FISSURE, and TISSUE. In words like PASSION, EX-PRESSION, and DISCUSSION, the sh sound is not indicated by s alone but by ssi. In PENSION, EXPANSION, and DIMENSION, the sh sound is in-dicated by si. Thus, you might have trouble deciding whether there is an s or a double s in words that end in –ion. You might also be uncertain about doubling the s when the next letter is u (ERASURE, PRESSURE).
    The letter s sometimes has the sound of zh rather than sh in words like ENCLOSURE and EXPOSURE. But the word will not be spelled with z unless there is a z in the basic word (SEIZE, SEIZURE).
    We will work on these problems, but first let's review the adding of endings. Try writing the indicated forms of the following words. In (e) and (f), the consonant is changed to an s, making the sh sound. (See Chapter 16 for more about the –ion ending.)

(a) disclose   _____ure   (d) compress   _____ion

(b) fuse   _____ion   (e) extrude   _____ion

(c) please   _____ure   (f) suspend   _____ion

– – – – – – – – – – – – – –

(a) disclosure; (b) fusion; (c) pleasure; (d) compression; (e) ex-trusion; (f) suspension

5. There are two ways to decide whether the s is doubled before –ure or –ion. If the vowel before the s is long, the s is not doubled before the ending. If the vowel is short, a double s follows. This is consistent with rules given in earlier chapters. In addition, you can be pretty sure the s is doubled if you can think of some other form of the word that ends in double s. Compare these words:

      expose, exposure   press, pressure

   A chain reaction to produce an _____ of a nuclear
                         (form of EXPLODE)

bomb might require the fis_____on of a heavy element such as uranium

or the fu_____on of a light element such as hydrogen.

– – – – – – – – – – – – – – –

   explosion, fission, fusion

6. Several words have the written combination sci to indicate the sound of sh. Some of these are:

      omniscient   conscious   conscience

   A number of words come from the Latin word for "know." One of them is SCIENCE. Others are:

(a) con_____ce

(b) con_____ous

(c) omni_____t

– – – – – – – – – – – – – –

   (a) conscience; (b) conscious; (c) omniscient

7. In Freudian psychology, the personality is divided into the superego,

the ego, and the id. The id is the unc_____or submerged por-
                       (not aware)

tion of the personality; the ego is the c_____ous or waking part;
                         (aware)

and the superego might be termed the con_____ence.
                     (little voice within)

– – – – – – – – – – – – – – –

   unconscious, conscious, conscience

8. Only a few words have the combination se to indicate the sound of sh.
The most common example is NAUSEOUS, although many people pronounce GASEOUS with the sh sound.

   The combination ti indicates the sound of sh in a great many words.
Most of these end in –tion, but others end in –tient, –tience, –tial, and
–tian. The –tian ending usually indicates nationality or citizenship, as
in CROATIAN. Some examples are:

>   quotient   impatience   palatial   Dalmatian

   After announcing that he had been in communication with

M_____, he suddenly found himself committed as a
(visitors from Mars)

pa_____t in a mental hospital.
   (inmate)

_ _ _ _ _ _ _ _ _ _ _ _ _ _

   Martians, patient

9. Riots have resulted from _____ or political
                                    (form of RACE)

_____ s in recent years. Cities have sometimes resorted
   (form of TENSE)

to mar_____ law when economic and so_____l _____ s
                                                        (form of PRESS)

have exploded into mob violence.

_ _ _ _ _ _ _ _ _ _ _ _ _ _

   racial, tensions, martial, social, pressures

SELF-TEST

Circle the misspelled words and write the correct spelling in the spaces beside them.

1. crustacian _____		11. disclozure _____	
2. mashine _____		12. expanssion _____	
3. ocean _____		13. promosion _____	
4. shagrin _____		14. discussion _____	
5. chivalry _____		15. fision _____	
6. social _____		16. dimention _____	
7. sharade _____		17. glacier _____	
8. suffitient _____		18. nausious _____	
9. crushial _____		19. fissure _____	
10. expresion _____		20. consious _____	

ANSWERS TO SELF-TEST

1. crustacean	11. disclosure
2. machine	12. expansion
4. chagrin	13. promotion
7. charade	15. fission
8. sufficient	16. dimension
9. crucial	18. nauseous
10. expression	20. conscious

CHAPTER 10

The Letter Saver

The nice thing about the apostrophe is that it is often used, but its name is rarely spelled. It is a letter saver because it is used to form <u>contractions</u> (that is, combined forms of words in which some letters are left out). Some examples are:

> can't for cannot   isn't for is not
> o'clock for of the clock   it's for it is

The apostrophe is also used in poetry to save syllables and make poetry scan—ne'er, e'en, o'er—but if you are a poet you already know that, and if you are not, you don't need to worry about it. (It is sometimes used to form plurals. See Chapter 6.)

1. The important thing to remember about the apostrophe in contractions is that it goes <u>exactly</u> where letters are left out. Here are some contractions with the apostrophe correctly placed:

would not	who is	they are	you had
o	i	a	ha
wouldn't	who's	they're	you'd

An infrequently used exception to the rule of exact placement of the apostrophe is the contraction SHAN'T for SHALL NOT. If the contraction were written SHA'N'T, the word would be too awkward, so one apostrophe is used. A much more common exception is WON'T for WILL NOT.

Write contractions for the following phrases:

(a) were not _____   (c) he is _____

(b) is not _____   (d) they are _____

- - - - - - - - - - - - - -

    (a) weren't; (b) isn't; (c) he's; (d) they're

2. You have to be careful because there are often other words that sound exactly like the contractions of certain phrases. What contractions sound like the following words?

(a) whose _____   (c) its   _____

(b) theirs _____   (d) their _____

- - - - - - - - - - - - - -

    (a) who's; (b) there's; (c) it's; (d) they're

3. The other use of the apostrophe is in forming the possessive: Aunt SARAH'S niece is JOHN'S wife. Possessives of singular words cause little trouble unless the last letter is <u>s</u>. Is it THOMAS' boat or THOMAS'S boat? There are different conventions about this situation, and both forms shown above are correct. The simplest course, and the one recommended here, is to use the form that most closely reflects the spoken word: JONAS'S bad luck is legendary. Most people would use three syllables for the possessive of JONAS, so write it JONAS'S.

    Mr. _____ students often heard him joke, "One
         (possessive of DAVIS)

_____ Mede is a history _____
    (possessive of MAN)   (possessive of STUDENT)
Persian."

- - - - - - - - - - - - - -

    Davis's or Davis' (depending on how you say it aloud), man's,
    student's

4. Possessives of plurals require a little more thought. If the plural does not end in <u>s</u>, just add '<u>s</u>: WOMEN'S apparel, FISHERMEN'S tales, SHEEP'S wool. If the plural ends in <u>s</u>, add only the apostrophe: old WIVES' tales, ANIMALS' instincts.

    Children_____ stories often portray princesses____ suitors as hand-
some princes changed into frogs or as knights on white horses.

- - - - - - - - - - - - - -

    children's, princesses'

5. If the possessive refers to more than one, add 's to the last word in the series only: John and MARY'S honeymoon; Tom, Dick, and HARRY'S adventure.

The College of William and Mary is sometimes called _____

and _____ College.

– – – – – – – – – – – – – – –

William and Mary's

6. The biggest single problem related to the apostrophe is caused by two little words that are frequently confused. When do you write IT'S and when ITS, and which is which? Pronouns form the possessive without the apostrophe; contractions always require it. Therefore, IT'S always means IT IS.

Insert apostrophes as required in the following sentence:

Its its own tail its eating.

– – – – – – – – – – – – – – –

It's its own tail it's eating.

7. Now try inserting apostrophes in this sentence:

Sometimes its not clear that virtue is its own reward.

– – – – – – – – – – – – – – –

Sometimes it's not clear that virtue is its own reward.

SELF-TEST

1. Add apostrophes as necessary in the following sentence:

   Its rumored that Sarah and Bills engagement has been called off, but their many friends theories cant be taken seriously until the rumors confirmed.

2. Write the possessives for the following words:

   (a) people   _____   (d) Andy   _____

   (b) men   _____   (e) babies   _____

   (c) children   _____   (f) governments   _____

3. Write the contractions for the following phrases:

   (a) will not   _____   (d) is not   _____

   (b) it is   _____   (e) are not   _____

   (c) could not   _____   (f) she is   _____

ANSWERS TO SELF-TEST

1. It's rumored that Sarah and Bill's engagement has been called off, but their many friends' theories can't be taken seriously until the rumor's confirmed.

2. (a) people's   (c) children's   (e) babies'
   (b) men's   (d) Andy's   (f) governments'

3. (a) won't   (c) couldn't   (e) aren't
   (b) it's   (d) isn't   (f) she's

CHAPTER 11

Beginnings

Something like 60 percent of all words in English are derived from Latin; a great many of these are made up of a prefix (from a Latin preposition) and a basic word or word part (a root from a Latin verb). A short course in Latin would make spelling easier, but since you probably have neither the time nor the inclination for that, let's see what help we can get from an examination of various prefixes.

Each prefix has several forms because of <u>euphony</u> (the tendency to change a sound to a more pleasing sound). DIFFER, for example, comes from the prefix <u>dis</u> and the verb <u>ferre</u>, and literally means "to carry apart." (FERRY comes from the same root.) For ease of pronunciation, <u>dis</u> became <u>dif</u>.

When the last letter of a prefix is the same as the first letter of the basic word or word part, you have a problem: to double or not to double. If you understand the prefixes and something about the root, this becomes less troublesome. The following is a list of prefixes and sample words derived from them. Study the way each prefix and root are combined. Understanding this, you will save yourself some "double" trouble.

LATIN PREFIXES

Prefix	Meaning	Variant Spelling	Sample Words
ab	from		abhor, abnormal, absent
ad	toward, to		admission, advocate, advertisement, advance
		a-	ascribe, aver
		ac-	access, accord
		af-	affect, affluent
		ag-	aggravate, aggregate
		al-	allot, alleviate
		an-	annex, announce
		ap-	appear, applaud
		ar-	arrest, arrive
		as-	assent, assign
		at-	attend, attest
ante	before		antecedent, anteroom
circum	around		circumstance, circumvent
con	with, together		conference, convocation
		co-	coordinate, cooperate
		col-	collapse, colleague
		com-	commerce, compose
		cor-	correlate, correspond
contra	against		contradict, contravene
de	down		depend, depose, detract
dis	from, away, apart		disease, disturb, dismantle, dismiss
		di-	digress, divert
		dif-	differ, diffuse

Prefix	Meaning	Variant Spelling	Sample Words
ex	out of, from		excerpt, extract
		e-	eject, evict
		ef-	efface, effect, effeminate
extra	beyond		extraneous, extradition extraordinary
		extro-	extrovert
in	in, into, on (with nouns and verbs)		incline, intrude, invent
		il-	illuminate
		im-	imbibe, import
		ir-	irradiate, irrigate
	not (with adjectives)		indecisive, inept, informal
		il-	illiterate, illegal
		ig-	ignoble, ignorant
		im-	immodest, improper
		ir-	irregular, irrational
inter	between		interfere, international, interact
intra	within		intramural, intravenous
		intro-	introspective, introvert
per	through		perceive, permit
pre	before		precaution, prescribe
pro	for, before, forth		procession, proclaim
post	after		postdate, postpone
re	back, again		react, reorganize, review

Prefix	Meaning	Variant Spelling	Sample Words
retro	backward		retrospect, retrograde, retroactive
sub	under, beneath		submarine, submerge, submit, subterfuge
		suc-	succumb, succinct
		suf-	suffix, suffer
		sug-	suggest
		sup-	supplant, suppose
		sur-	surreptitious, surrogate
		sus-	suspend, suspect
super	over, above		superimpose, supernational, supersede
trans	across		transact, translate, transpose
		tra-	traverse
ultra	beyond		ultramarine, ultramodern

The foregoing Latin prefixes account for the great majority of words formed from a root plus a prefix. There are a number of Greek prefixes as well, but the main one that causes trouble is anti, which means "against." (Some examples are: ANTICLIMAX, ANTIDOTE, and ANTIFREEZE.) The Greek anti causes problems because of the confusion with the Latin ante, which means "before" (as in ANTE BELLUM and ANTEDILUVIAN). If the sense of the word is "against," spell it anti. If the gist of the meaning is "before," spell it ante.

This might be a good time for a rest, before you return to the task of working with some of the prefixes.

1. Combine the following prefixes and roots. Remember that the spelling of the prefix might change when it is combined with the root. (In all of these exercises, refer to the list of prefixes and sample words whenever necessary.)

> Examples: ab + normal   abnormal
>   ad + fect   affect

(a) ab + olish   _____

(b) ad + duce   _____

(c) ad + nounce   _____

(d) ante + cedent   _____

(e) circum + scribe _____

- - - - - - - - - - - - - -

   (a) abolish; (b) adduce; (c) announce; (d) antecedent; (e) circum-
   scribe

2. Combine the following prefixes and roots, changing the spelling of the prefix as necessary:

(a) con + tribute   _____

(b) con + league   _____

(c) contra + diction _____

(d) de + parture   _____

(e) dis + turb   _____

(f) dis + vert   _____

(g) dis + ferent   _____

- - - - - - - - - - - - - -

   (a) contribute; (b) colleague; (c) contradiction; (d) departure;
   (e) disturb; (f) divert; (e) different

3. Combine the following prefixes and roots:

(a) ex + cavate   _____

(b) ex + liminate   _____

(c) ex + fect   _____

(d) extra + territorial _____

(e) extra + vagant   _____

(f) extra + vert   _____

- - - - - - - - - - - - - -

(a) excavate; (b) eliminate; (c) effect; (d) extraterritorial;
(e) extravagant; (f) extrovert

Note: EXTROVERT is the only change in spelling of the prefix
extra- to extro-. Be sure to write EXTROVERT and EXTRO-
VERSION.

4. Combine the following prefixes and roots:

(a) in + volve   _____

(b) in + rigate   _____

(c) in + oculate   _____

(d) in + competent   _____

(e) in + legible   _____

(f) in + regular   _____

- - - - - - - - - - - - - - -

(a) involve; (b) irrigate; (c) inoculate; (d) incompetent; (e) illegible;
(f) irregular

Note: If some of these combinations seem strange, remember that
sometimes in- means "in" or "into" and sometimes it means "not."

5. Combine the following prefixes and roots:

(a) inter + racial   _____

(b) inter + action   _____

(c) intra + mural   _____

(d) intra + vert   _____

(e) intra + spective _____

(a) interracial; (b) interaction; (c) intramural; (d) introvert;
(e) introspective

Note: Did you double the r in INTERRACIAL? Also note that the
change of spelling from intra- to intro- is fairly common (for example
INTRODUCE).

6. Combine the following prefixes and roots:

(a) per + ception   _____

(b) pre + scription   _____

(c) pre + ference   _____

(d) pro + clamation   _____

(e) pro + nunciation   _____

(f) post + ponement   _____

(g) post + graduate   _____

(a) perception; (b) prescription; (c) preference; (d) proclamation;
(e) pronunciation; (f) postponement; (g) postgraduate

Note: Were you careful not to double the f in PREFERENCE?

7. Combine the following prefixes and roots:

(a) re + duction   _____

(b) re + fuge   _____

(c) retro + active   _____

(d) sub + terranean   _____

(e) sub + cess   _____

(f) sub + ficient   _____

(g) sub + pension   _____

(h) super + sede   _____

(i) super + impose   _____

(j) trans + fer   _____

(k) trans + gression   _____

(l) ultra + violet   _____

(m) ultra + sonic   _____

- - - - - - - - - - - - - - -

(a) reduction; (b) refuge; (c) retroactive; (d) subterranean;
(e) success; (f) sufficient; (g) suspension; (h) supersede;
(i) superimpose; (j) transfer; (k) transgression; (l) ultraviolet;
(m) ultrasonic

Now that you have studied the chart of prefixes and worked with them in several exercises, you are ready to study a list of the main words in which a double letter occurs because the last letter of the prefix is the same as the first letter of the root. The list is long; resist the tendency to read through it rapidly. The purpose in having you study the list is to help you see the actual structure of each word.

Have a pencil handy as you study the words and either mark lightly the division between each prefix and root or at least touch the paper at the point of division to help your concentration. If the spelling of the word seems strange, it would be a good idea to look up the word in the dictionary to see how it was derived.

Many of the words you are about to examine result from the negative prefix in- or its variations for euphony, il-, im-, and ir-. The prefix in- also means "in," "into," or "on." Whatever the prefix, a double letter results only if the last letter of the prefix is the same as the first letter of the root.

Here, then, are some of the main words that have a double letter near the beginning.

abbreviate	allergy	appropriate
accede	alleviate	approve
accelerate	alliance	arrangement
accent	allocate	arrival
acceptable	allot	arrogance
accessible	allowance	assail
accessory	allusion	assassin
accidentally	ammunition	assault
acclaim	annex	assent
acclamation	annihilate	assess
acclimate	anniversary	asset
accommodate	announcement	assignment
accompaniment	annoyance	assistance
accomplice	annual	associate
accomplish	annuity	assort
according	annul	assume
accordion	annulled	assurance
accost	apparatus	attach
accountant	apparel	attain
accredit	apparent	attempt
accrue	appeal	attendance
accumulate	appearance	attention
accuracy	appetite	attest
affable	applaud	attitude
affect	appliance	attorney
affiliate	applicant	collaborator
affluence	apply	collage
affront	appointment	collapsible
aggravate	appraisal	collar
aggressive	appreciable	collate
aggressor	appreciate	collateral
allay	apprehend	colleague
allegiance	approach	

collector
college
collegiate
collide
collision
colloquial
collusion
command
commemorate
commence
commendable
commensurate
commentary
commentator
commercial
commiserate
commissary
commission
commitment
committee
commodity
common
communicate
communism
community
connect
connive
connoisseur
connotation
correct
correlate
correspondence
corridor
corroborate
corrode
corrosion
corrugated
corruptible

difference
difficult
dissatisfied
dissect
dissemble
dissension
dissidence

dissimilar
dissipate
dissociate
dissolute
dissolve
dissuade

eccentric
ecclesiastical
effect
effeminate
effervescent
effete
efficiency
effrontery
ellipse

illegal
illegible
illegitimate
illicit
illiteracy
illiterate
illogical
illuminate
illusion
illusive
illusory
illustrator
illustrious
immaculate
immaterial
immature
immeasurable
immediate
immemorial
immense
immerse
immigrant
imminent
immobile
immoderate
immodest
immolate
immoral
immortal

immovable
immune
immunity
immutable
innate
innervate
innocence
innocuous
innovator
innuendo
innumerable
irrational
irreconcilable
irredeemable
irrefutable
irregular
irrelevant
irreligious
irreparable
irreplaceable
irreproachable
irresistible
irresponsible
irreverence
irrevocable
irrigate
irritable
irritant

misshapen
misspell
misstate
misstep

suffice
sufficient
suffix
suffocate
suffrage
suffuse
suggestible
supplant
supplementary
supply
supportable
suppose

supposition	surrealism	surrogate
suppository	surrender	surround
suppressible	surreptitious	

Because so many words have double letters in them, there is a strong tendency to double letters even when there is no reason for it. This trend in spelling is particularly strong when the prefix is <u>in-</u>, since so many words beginning with this prefix actually have a double <u>n</u>. Thus, a great many people fall into error when they come to a word like INOCU-LATE.

When you give someone a shot, you INOCULATE him. If you had only a smattering of Latin and not much word history, you might think INOCU-LATE originally meant something like "a shot in the eye," since the Latin <u>oculus</u> means "eye" and is the source of words such as OCULIST, BINOCULARS, and MONOCLE. But <u>oculus</u> also means "bud," and the original meaning of INOCULATE was "to graft by budding." Needless to say, you don't have to be an etymologist to avoid errors such as spelling INOCULATE with two <u>n</u>'s. You only have to be careful. (But also be careful with INNOCUOUS, which comes from a different Latin root and does have two <u>n</u>'s.)

The following list contains a large number of words that do <u>not</u> have double letters near the beginning. Many of these words may not be problem words for you, but each word on the list is misspelled by many people. (Don't be concerned if many of these words are new to you; many of them are familiar only to specialists in a particular area.) Concentrate on the words you already recognize, and use this list for later reference. Then try the exercise that follows.

abandon	almanac	anatomy
abet	almighty	apartment
abolish	almost	apologize
abridge	already	apostle
abrupt	although	arithmetic
abundance	altogether	arouse
abuse	aluminum	ascend
abysmal	always	aspirin
abyss	amenable	
academic	amiable	colic
acoustics	amicable	coliseum
adapt	amoral	comedian
adept	amorous	conical
agonize	analysis	conifer
agreeable	analyze	coronation

coronet

disagreeable
disappearance
disappoint
disarray
disaster
disastrous
disburse
discard
discernible
disciple
disciplinary
discomfort
disconcert
discordant
discount
discourteous
discovery
discreet
discrepancy
discrete
discretion
discriminate
discus
discuss
disdainful
disease
disguise
disheveled
dishonest
disillusion
disinfectant
dismal
dismantle
dismissal
disparagement

disparate
disparity
dispensary
disperse
dispirited*
disposal
disposition
dispossess
disputable
disruption
distance
distasteful
distillery
distinct
distinguishable
distortion
distraught
distress
distribute
district
disturbance

eclipse
economical
ecstasy
eczema
elapse
elated
elegance
elementary
elevator
elicit
eligible
eliminate
elite
eloquence
elude

elusive

imagery
imaginary
inane
inebriated
inedible
ineligible
inert
inertia
inevitable
inimitable
initial
initiative
inoculate
inundate
irascible
irate
iridescent
ironic
irony

misanthrope
miserable
mishap
mismanage
misnomer

sublimate
sublime
subliminal
subordinate
suburb
suburban
sugar
supremacy
supreme

---

*By the rules, you would expect this word to have <u>ss</u>, but it does not.

8. We don't have the space to include practice exercises for all the words in the lists you have just studied. If you miss any words in this exercise, review other words with similar spelling problems. When you're ready, go on to the Self-Test. For a thorough test of this chapter, have a friend ask you to spell the words on both lists.

Circle the twelve words in the following paragraph that are misspelled and correct the spelling:

Many men of good will felt they had to abbandon all

eforts to abolish slavery in the aggonizing period before

the Civil War. A few spoke out with elloquence against

the dissturbing abbuses practiced on some plantations,

pointing out that slavery was a dissease afecting all of

society, black and white. Those who kept silent were

not imoral, but they were affraid of the social and eccono-

mic pressures that might be exerted against them, and

their fears were far from immaginary.

----

abandon, efforts, agonizing, eloquence, disturbing, abuses, disease, affecting, immoral, afraid, economic, imaginary

SELF-TEST

Circle each misspelled word below and write the correct spelling in the space beside it.

1.	abandon		18.	dissheveled
2.	abreviate		19.	aparatus
3.	acceptable		20.	approach
4.	afront		21.	agressor
5.	inocuous		22.	appologize
6.	abbundance		23.	disastrous
7.	accoustics		24.	inoculate
8.	adapt		25.	irridescent
9.	colaborator		26.	supplement
10.	comedian		27.	efficient
11.	appreciate		28.	allmighty
12.	comentary		29.	ellusive
13.	disspirited		30.	disease
14.	imigrate		31.	appetite
15.	immodest		32.	immobile
16.	misshapen		33.	acumulate
17.	disimilar		34.	apostle

ANSWERS TO SELF-TEST

2.	abbreviate		17.	dissimilar
4.	affront		18.	disheveled
5.	innocuous		19.	apparatus
6.	abundance		21.	aggressor
7.	acoustics		22.	apologize
9.	collaborator		25.	iridescent
12.	commentary		28.	almighty
13.	dispirited		29.	elusive
14.	immigrate		33.	accumulate

Part Three

This part concentrates on a perennial spelling problem—endings. We've already discussed the general rules of ways to add the ending including when to drop the e and when to double the final consonant. (See Part 1.) But what about the ending itself? Is is STATIONARY or STATION-ERY? MISCHIEVIOUS or MISCHIEVOUS? COMPATABLE or COMPAT-IBLE? Each chapter in this part covers a different set of endings; because the chapters can be read in any order, you may want to look first at the endings which give you particular difficulty.

There are no absolute rules for telling which ending is correct, but there are guidelines that will help you cut down your margin for error. Using these guidelines, when you complete this part you should be able to identify incorrect spellings and choose the correct endings for most common words with these endings:

- -ary, -ery;
- -able, -ible, -uble;
- -ize, -yze, -ise;
- -ious, -eous, -ous, -ius, -us;
- -sion, -tion;
- -ant, -ent;
- -ify, -efy;
- -er, -or, -eer, -ier, -eur, -euse;
- -ceed, -cede, -sede.

You will also be able to identify and correctly spell some of the major exceptions to these guidelines. In addition, while you are learning about endings, you will get a lot of useful practice spelling the other parts of problem words.

Many of the words in these chapters will be new to you. The word lists are as complete as possible; you aren't expected to know all of the words. Study the spelling of words you already know, and use this part as a reference later.

CHAPTER 12

The Quandary About
-*ary* and -*ery*

It would be nice if most of the words discussed in this chapter ended in
-ary while only a few ended in -ery (or the other way around). Then you
could just memorize the short list and know that all the other words had
the other ending. Unfortunately, the two endings occur with about the
same frequency, with maybe a few more words in the -ary list.

Even so, a look at the two lists (pages 107-108) will reveal a fairly
helpful guide to the proper ending. If the word contains a smaller related word—complete and unchanged—within it, and if the word is a noun,
the ending is probably -ery. Consider CREAM in CREAMERY, HATCH
in HATCHERY, and REFINE in REFINERY. Some -ary words contain
smaller words within them, but the -ary words are mostly adjectives,
such as DOCUMENTARY and SECONDARY. If a smaller related word
cannot be found within the longer word, the ending is probably -ary.
Words meeting this requirement include ARBITRARY, COROLLARY, and
OBITUARY.

Of the words in the -ary list, most are <u>adjectives</u> (although some of
these are also used as nouns). Of the words in the -ery list, almost all
are <u>nouns</u>.

1. If a longer word has a smaller related word within it, it probably

ends in _____.
           (-ary/-ery)

- - - - - - - - - - - - - -

   -ery

2. If an -ary/-ery word is an adjective, the correct spelling is most

likely _____ .
         (-ary/-ery)

- - - - - - - - - - - - - -

   -ary

3. If such a word is a noun, the chances are very good that it ends in

_____ .

   (-ary/-ery)

– – – – – – – – – – – – – –

   -ery

4. Here are the main -ary and -ery words. As you study these lists,
think about the guidelines just presented.

<u>-ary</u>

arbitrary	mercenary
auxiliary	momentary
beneficiary	necessary
binary	obituary
boundary	ordinary
commentary	parliamentary
commissary	penitentiary
complementary	precautionary
complimentary	preliminary
contemporary	primary
corollary	quandary
culinary	reactionary
disciplinary	revolutionary
dispensary	rudimentary
documentary	sanctuary
elementary	sanitary
evolutionary	secondary
extraordinary	sedentary
fiduciary	sedimentary
fragmentary	solitary
hereditary	stationary (still)
imaginary	statuary
infirmary	summary
inflationary	supplementary
judiciary	temporary
legendary	tributary
library	veterinary

-ery

adultery	haberdashery
bindery	hatchery
bravery	imagery
brewery	machinery
bribery	nunnery
cannery	nursery
cemetery	ornery
confectionery	periphery
creamery	recovery
crockery	refinery
cutlery	scullery
delivery	shimmery
discovery	skullduggery
effrontery	slippery
embroidery	snobbery
finery	stationery (paper)
foppery	summery (like summer)
forgery	treachery
greenery	

Supply the proper endings of the following words:

(a) arbitr_____

(b) extraordin_____

(c) brav_____

(d) crock_____

(e) libr_____

(f) prelimin_____

(g) periph_____

(h) embroid_____

- - - - - - - - - - - - - -

(a) arbitrary; (b) extraordinary; (c) bravery; (d) crockery;
(e) library; (f) preliminary; (g) periphery; (h) embroidery

5. The inspector from the Health Department felt that a tempor_____
injunction against the cann_____ was necess_____, since the
management had provided only the most rudiment_____ sanit_____
facilities.

- - - - - - - - - - - - -

temporary, cannery, necessary, rudimentary, sanitary

6. The young man's business sense was certainly not imagin_____;
in only a few years he had acquired a station_____ store, a haber-
dash_____, and a hatch_____, and had even established a
book bind_____.

_ _ _ _ _ _ _ _ _ _ _ _ _ _

   imaginary, stationery, haberdashery, hatchery, bindery

SELF-TEST

Circle the misspelled words and write the correct spelling in the spaces beside them.

1. corollary _____
2. evolutionery _____
3. forgery _____
4. hereditery _____
5. infirmary _____
6. machinary _____
7. mercenery _____
8. nursery _____
9. parliamentery _____
10. quandery _____
11. reactionery _____
12. recovery _____
13. refinary _____
14. sanctuary _____
15. secondary _____
16. sedentery _____
17. tributery _____
18. treachery _____
19. veterinary _____

ANSWERS TO SELF-TEST

2. evolutionary
4. hereditary
6. machinery
7. mercenary
9. parliamentary

10. quandary
11. reactionary
13. refinery
16. sedentary
17. tributary

CHAPTER 13
Trouble with *-able* and *-ible*

Spelling would be a lot easier if there were not so many adjectives formed from verbs by adding the endings -able and -ible.[*] If you just decided to forget the problem and always end the word in -able, you would be right about two-thirds of the time, but two out of three is not enough if you want to be a good speller.

A third ending, -uble, appears in only a few words: SOLUBLE; its negative, INSOLUBLE; its cousin, INDISSOLUBLE; and VOLUBLE. In all these words, the u is sounded, thus removing all doubt about the proper ending.

The other words in this chapter do not have such clearly sounded vowels; thus, we must study them to find guidelines that will help us spell them. On the following pages are two lists of words: the first, words ending in -able; the second, those ending in -ible. The -able list is quite long (even though many words have been left out), but the list does give the main words that might cause trouble. Sometimes both the word and its negative are given, sometimes just one or the other. This is no problem because adding the negative prefix (usually in- or un-) does not change the basic word. Pay attention to the endings (-able and -ible) as you study the words. Check off the words you realize you normally misspell and words whose endings surprise you.

After you have studied the word lists, we will examine some of the words in an attempt to establish some general rules and some memory aids to help you keep the rules straight.

---

[*]There are a few nouns that resemble these adjectives, but they are from different sources. The main ones are CHASUBLE, CRUCIBLE, MANDIBLE, VEGETABLE, and BIBLE.

Words Ending in -able

acceptable
adaptable
adjustable
advisable
affable
agreeable
allowable
amenable
amiable
amicable
arguable
available
avoidable

bearable
believable
breakable

capable
changeable
comfortable
commendable
communicable
companionable
comparable
conceivable
considerable
culpable
curable

damageable
debatable
delectable
demonstrable
dependable
deplorable
desirable
despicable
detachable
detectable
detestable
disagreeable
disputable
distinguishable

durable

educable
employable
enforceable
enjoyable
enviable
equitable
eradicable
exchangeable
excitable
excusable
expendable
explainable

fashionable
favorable
flammable
forseeable
forgettable
forgivable
formidable

governable

habitable
honorable
hospitable

imaginable
immeasurable
immovable
immutable
impassable
impeccable
impenetrable
impermeable
imperturbable
implacable
impregnable
improbable
inadvisable
inalienable
incalculable
incomparable

incurable
indefatigable
indispensable
indomitable
ineffable
inevitable
inexorable
inexplicable
inflammable
inimitable
innumerable
insatiable
inscrutable
inseparable
insufferable
insurmountable
interminable
invariable
irreconcilable
irredeemable
irrefutable
irreparable
irreplaceable
irreproachable
irrevocable
irritable

justifiable

knowable
knowledgeable

lamentable
laudable
laughable
liable
likable
livable
lovable

malleable
manageable
marriageable
measurable
memorable

mentionable
miserable

navigable
negotiable
notable
noticeable

objectionable
obtainable
operable

palatable
palpable
pardonable
passable
payable
peaceable
perceivable
perishable
personable
pitiable
pliable
practicable
predictable
preferable
presentable
probable
profitable
pronounceable

provable
publishable
punishable

readable
reasonable
receivable
recoverable
rectifiable
redeemable
refutable
regrettable
reliable
remarkable
removable
repairable
repayable
reputable
resolvable
retainable
retractable
returnable

salable
salvageable
seizable
separable
serviceable
shakable

sizable
solvable
stretchable

tarnishable
taxable
teachable
tolerable
touchable
traceable
trainable
transferable
treasonable
treatable

unbelievable
uncontrollable
undeniable
unmistakable
untenable
unthinkable
usable

valuable
variable
viable
vulnerable

workable

Words Ending in –ible

accessible
admissible
audible

combustible
compatible
comprehensible
contemptible
convertible
convincible
corruptible
credible

deductible

defensible
destructible
digestible
dirigible
discernible

edible
eligible
expansible
expressible

fallible
feasible
flexible

forcible

gullible

illegible
imperceptible
impossible
inaccessible
inadmissible
imcomprehensible
incorrigible
incredible
indefensible
indelible

inedible	legible	reversible
ineligible	negligible	seducible
inexhaustible		sensible
inexpressible	ostensible	suggestible
infallible	perceptible	suppressible
inflexible	perfectible	susceptible
intangible	permissible	
invincible	plausible	tangible
invisible		
irascible	reducible	unintelligible
irresistible	reprehensible	visible
irresponsible		

The words in the preceding lists were formed by adding an ending to a basic word which might have been a verb (ADAPTABLE, FLEXIBLE), a verb with the final letter changed or eliminated (CURABLE, RELIABLE), or some other word part (CREDIBLE, VULNERABLE). It is often helpful to study these words by considering the letter preceding the ending (-able or -ible), since the spelling of the ending might be related to this final letter of the basic word part.

- If the last letter of the word part (that is, the letter preceding the ending) is a vowel (a, e, i, o, u, w, or y), the ending is always -able: CHANGEABLE, RELIABLE, ALLOWABLE, and PAYABLE.*

- If the last letter of the word part is b, the ending is always -able: PROBABLE, IMPERTUBABLE.

- If the last letter of the word part is hard c, (sounds like k), the ending is always -able: AMICABLE, EDUCABLE.

- If the last letter of the word part is f, the ending is always able: AFFABLE.

- If the last letter of the word part is hard g (sounds like guh), the ending is always -able: INDEFATIGABLE, NAVIGABLE.

- If the last letter of the word part is h in a combination such as ch, gh, and sh, the ending is always -able: STRETCHABLE, LAUGHABLE, PUNISHABLE.

- If the last letter of the word part is k, the ending is always -able: BREAKABLE, LIKABLE.

- If the last letter of the word part is m, the ending is always -able: FLAMMABLE, REDEEMABLE.

---

*In practice, the vowels a and o never precede the ending.

- If the last letter of the word part is <u>n</u>, the ending is almost always -able: AMENABLE, TENABLE. (The single common exception is DISCERNIBLE.)

- If the last letter of the word part is <u>p</u>, the ending is always -able: CULPABLE, PALPABLE.

- If the last letter of the word part is <u>r</u>, the ending is always -able: DURABLE, IMPENETRABLE.

- If the last letter of the word part is <u>v</u>, the ending is always -able: BELIEVABLE, PROVABLE.*

- If the last letter of the word part is <u>z</u>, the ending is always -able: SEIZABLE, SIZABLE.

In summary, you can be sure that the ending is -able if the last letter of the word part is any one of the following: a vowel, <u>b</u>, hard <u>c</u>, <u>f</u>, hard <u>g</u>, <u>h</u>, <u>k</u>, <u>m</u>, <u>n</u>, <u>p</u>, <u>r</u>, <u>v</u>, or <u>z</u>. You should memorize the list of letters that are always followed by -able. Since words are easier to remember than letters, memorize this sentence:

> Mr. Able's zoo includes bears, cows, foxes, nanny goats, horses, kangeroos, mice, pigs, rats, vampire bats, and zebras.

<u>Every</u> word in that sentence begins with a letter that is always followed by -able. But be careful in the cases of hard <u>c</u> and hard <u>g</u>. COW and GOAT begin with the hard sounds of those initial letters, but soft <u>c</u> and soft <u>g</u> are always followed by -ible.

Do not go on until you have memorized the sentence about Mr. Able's zoo.

1. Write the sentence you have been asked to memorize.

_ _ _ _ _ _ _ _ _ _ _ _ _ _

Mr. Able's zoo includes bears, cows, foxes, nanny goats, horses, kangeroos, mice, pigs, rats, vampire bats, and zebras. (Remember that <u>n</u> has one exception: DISCERNIBLE.)

---

*Note that in all these words, the final <u>e</u> of the basic word is dropped before the ending is added. If you need review on dropping <u>e</u> before the ending, see Chapter 2.

2. Write the -ble forms of the following words, applying the guidelines given on pages 114-115.

(a) navigate _____   (i) ineff- _____

(b) culp- _____   (j) imperturb- _____

(c) presume _____   (k) prove _____

(d) peace _____   (l) value _____

(e) laugh _____   (m) insure _____

(f) break _____   (n) implac- _____

(g) size _____   (o) allow _____

(h) practice _____   (p) certify _____

- - - - - - - - - - - - - - - -

(a) navigable; (b) culpable; (c) presumable; (d) peaceable; (e) laughable; (f) breakable; (g) sizable; (h) practicable (note the change from soft to hard c); (i) ineffable; (j) imperturbable; (k) provable; (l) valuable; (m) insurable; (n) implacable; (o) allowable; (p) certifiable (Remember that y is changed to i.)

Note: In many of these words, e was dropped before adding -able. However, words such as PEACE and CHANGE, which end with a soft c or g sound, often retain the silent e. You may want to review these rules in Chapters 2 and 4.

A few words in frame 2 (PEACEABLE, VALUABLE, ALLOWABLE) are not consistent with the memory aid about Mr. Able's zoo. They are examples of the rule that a vowel is followed by -able, and remember that w and y are sometimes vowels.

If you plan to stop pretty soon, this is a good place for a break.

Here are some more guidelines:

- If the last letter of the stem is soft c (sounds like s), the ending is always –ible: FORCIBLE,* IRASCIBLE.

- If the last letter of the stem is soft g (sounds like j), the ending is always –ible: INCORRIGIBLE, NEGLIGIBLE.

- If the word part ends in ns, the ending is probably –ible: COMPREHENSIBLE, RESPONSIBLE.

- If the stem ends in ss, the ending is –ible, with very few exceptions: ADMISSIBLE, POSSIBLE; but PASSABLE, IMPASSABLE.

There is no reliable rule when the word part ends in d, l, t, or x. Refer to the word lists to check words that give you trouble and learn them individually.

3. Write the –ble forms of the following words:

(a) mention _____   (e) sink _____

(b) poss– _____   (f) discern _____

(c) amen– _____   (g) forc– _____

(d) enforce _____   (h) neglig– _____

- - - - - - - - - - - - - -

   (a) mentionable; (b) possible; (c) amenable; (d) enforceable;*
   (e) sinkable; (f) discernible; (g) forcible;* (h) negligible

The rules discussed so far in this chapter are summarized in the following table.

---

*Compare the spellings of FORCIBLE and ENFORCEABLE. Neither word violates any of the rules given in this book, although one or the other is an apparent exception. However, FORC– is a word part ending in soft c, while ENFORCE is a complete word ending in silent e. FORC–IBLE means "by force," while FORCEABLE means "able to be forced." Because of the difference in meanings, there are different spellings.

Word Part Ends With	Ending	Examples	Exceptions
vowel	–able	changeable reliable arguable allowable payable	none
b	–able	probable	none
hard c	–able	amicable educable	none
f	–able	ineffable	none
hard g	–able	indefatigable navigable	none
h	–able	stretchable laughable punishable	none
k	–able	breakable likable	none
m	–able	flammable redeemable	none
n	–able	amenable tenable	discernible
p	–able	culpable palpable	none
r	–able	durable impenetrable	none
v	–able	believable provable	none
z	–able	seizable sizable	none
soft c	–ible	forcible irascible	none
soft g	–ible	incorrigible negligible	none
ns	–ible	comprehensible responsible	none
ss	–ible	admissible possible	none

If that last-letter-before-the-ending approach is not for you, another method of attack might make sense to you. All these words are combinations of word part plus ending (-able or -ible). Some general rules can be discovered (although there are exceptions) by studying the <u>structure</u> of the word part rather than just its final letter. Since the -able words form the larger group, study them first.

The <u>-able</u> <u>Rules</u>

- If the word part is a full word (including words in which the final <u>e</u> is dropped before the ending), the ending is probably -able:

acceptable	detestable	peaceable
available	describable	perishable
avoidable	desirable	pleasurable
believable	discreditable	predictable
breakable	drinkable	presentable
changeable	enforceable	presumable
comfortable	excitable	profitable
commendable	excusable	readable
companionable	fashionable	seasonable
considerable	favorable	sizable
creditable	laughable	taxable
debatable	likable	thinkable
dependable	lovable	usable
deplorable	noticeable	valuable
detectable	passable	workable

- If the word part ends in <u>i</u> (the basic word might have ended with <u>y</u>), the ending is always -able, since there are no words ending in -iible:

appreciable	justifiable
dutiable	reliable
enviable	sociable

• If there is some other form of the word part that ends in
  –ate or –ation (DURATION, INFLAMMATION, PENE-
  TRATE, IMITATE), the ending is probably –able:

durable	inimitable	inviolable
flammable	innumerable	irreparable
impenetrable	inseparable	irritable
impregnable	intolerable	tolerable
inflammable		

4. Write the –ble forms of the following words:

(a) certify _____   (e) identify _____

(b) irritate _____   (f) separate _____

(c) envy _____   (g) duty _____

(d) communicate _____   (h) revoke _____

– – – – – – – – – – – – – – –

(a) certifiable; (b) irritable; (c) enviable; (d) communicable;
(e) identifiable; (f) separable; (g) dutiable; (h) revocable (note that
<u>k</u> becomes <u>c</u>)

The –ible Rules

• If the word part is not a full word (give or take a final <u>e</u>),
  the ending is probably –ible:

audible	feasible	irascible
combustible	forcible	negligible
compatible	horrible	plausible
credible	incorrigible	tangible
dirigible	indelible	terrible
divisible	infallible	visible
edible	intelligible	

5. Add the –ble endings to the following word parts:

(a) aud– _____ (g) dirig– _____

(b) compat– _____ (h) divis– _____

(c) ed– _____ (i) tang– _____

(d) debat– _____ (j) sens– _____

(e) compress– _____ (k) admiss– _____

(f) impass– _____ (l) imponder– _____

– – – – – – – – – – – – – –

(a) audible; (b) compatible; (c) edible; (d) debatable; (e) compress-
ible; (f) impassable; (g) dirigible; (h) divisible; (i) tangible;
(j) sensible; (k) admissible; (l) imponderable

The –ible Rules (continued)

- If a noun can be formed from the verb by adding –ion rather
  than –tion (ACCESSION comes from ACCESS), the ending
  is probably –ible. Note that this rule includes words like
  CONNECTION and DIGESTION, since adding –tion would
  cause them to be incorrectly spelled CONNECTTION and
  DIGESTTION.

accessible	contractible*	inexhaustible
affectible	convertible	perfectible
collectible	corruptible	suggestible
connectible	digestible	

- If the word part ends in soft c or soft g, the ending is probably –ible:

conducible	incorrigible	legible
convincible	intangible	negligible
deducible	intelligible	producible
eligible	invincible	reducible
forcible	irascible	seducible
illegible		

---

*But note RETRACTABLE.

6. Add the –ble endings to the following word parts:

(a) collect– _____   (e) retract– _____

(b) prob– _____   (f) suggest– _____

(c) digest– _____   (g) invinc– _____

(d) leg– _____   (h) tang– _____

- - - - - - - - - - - - - - -

(a) collectible; (b) probable; (c) digestible; (d) legible; (e) retractable; (f) suggestible; (g) invincible; (h) tangible

SELF-TEST

Circle each word that is misspelled and write the correct spelling in the space beside it.

1. amiable _____

2. combustable _____

3. contemptible _____

4. convertable _____

5. delectible _____

6. destructible _____

7. educable _____

8. flexible _____

9. formidable _____

10. immutible _____

11. inadvisable _____

12. inexplicible _____

13. insurmountable _____

14. invisable _____

15. irresponsible _____

16. marriagable _____

17. miserable _____

18. passible _____

19. peacable _____

20. permissible _____

21. punishible _____

22. reducible _____

23. salable _____

24. separible _____

ANSWERS TO SELF-TEST

2. combustible	16. marriageable
4. convertible	18. passable
5. delectable	19. peaceable
10. immutable	21. punishable
12. inexplicable	24. separable
14. invisible	

CHAPTER 14

Size up *-ize, -yze,* and *-ise*

Almost anyone who had to take a spelling test consisting only of words with the endings –ize, –yze, and –ise would miss a few of them, and a great many people would miss more than a few. In Great Britian, this particular group of words would be no trouble at all because just about all the –ize words are spelled –ise. Since you are stuck with American English, however, some study is in order.

1.   The list of –yze words is so short that it can be memorized. Then you can concentrate on the –ize and –ise endings. The –yze words are:

analyze	catalyze
paralyze	electrolyze
psychoanalyze	

In other forms of these words, the z becomes s (for example, ANALYSIS, CATALYST, ELECTROLYSIS, PARALYSIS, and PSYCHOANALYSIS). This change also occurs in –ize words (for example, CRITICIZE and CRITICISM).

The neurosurgeon tried in vain to ana_____ the cause of his patient's trouble. The man's right leg was para_____d, and there seemed to be no physical reason for it.

– – – – – – – – – – – – – –

analyze, paralyzed

2. There are relatively few words ending in -ise. Almost all of these words are formed by a word part plus -ise and do not have shorter forms that are complete words. The main -ise words are:

advertise	demise	exorcise
advise	despise	franchise
apprise	devise	revise
chastise	disguise	supervise
comprise	excise	surmise
compromise	exercise	surprise

Although he d_____ politicians and disapproved of the
                    (hated)

so-called art of compr_____, he was a responsible citizen and
                    (bargaining)

never failed to exer_____ his fran_____ at the polling place.
                (use)   (vote)

— — — — — — — — — — — — — —

despised, compromise, exercise, franchise

3. The great majority of verbs covered in this chapter end in -ize. The following list by no means includes all of them, but most of the words in common use are given.

aggrandize	harmonize	revitalize
agonize	homogenize	sanitize
amortize	hypnotize	scandalize
antagonize	italicize	scrutinize
apologize	legalize	sensitize
authorize	liberalize	serialize
baptize	magnetize	solemnize
brutalize	memorize	specialize
capsize	mesmerize	stabilize
cauterize	modernize	standardize
civilize	nationalize	subsidize
criticize	neutralize	summarize
crystallize	notarize	symbolize
deputize	organize	sympathize
emphasize	patronize	synchronize
energize	penalize	tantalize
epitomize	proselytize	theorize
equalize	publicize	tranquilize
familiarize	pulverize	unionize
formalize	realize	utilize
fraternize	recognize	verbalize
generalize		

A final note may help you with the words in this category. Most of the words in the –ize list follow a form that can be applied to other –ize words. If the word comes from an existing noun or adjective, the ending is almost certain to be –ize.

There is a growing tendency in industry and government to coin new verbs for special purposes. One might FINALIZE a contract, COM-PUTERIZE a manufacturing operation, or TRANSISTORIZE an electrical circuit. Many dictionaries do not yet reflect such usages, but they are words, nevertheless, and they all end in –ize.

Write the word that fits each of the following definitions:

(a) Assess a penalty   pena_____

(b) Form crystals   cryst_____

(c) Crush into powder   pulv_____

(d) Tip over a boat   caps_____

(e) Examine carefully   scrut_____

(f) Construct a theory   theor_____

— — — — — — — — — — — — — —

(a) penalize; (b) crystallize; (c) pulverize; (d) capsize; (e) scrutin-ize; (f) theorize

SELF-TEST

Complete the word suggested by each of the following definitions.

1.	Ask for forgiveness or admit error	apolo_____
2.	Empower, or give permission to act	auth_____
3.	Christen in religious ceremony	bap_____
4.	Stress or make a point strongly	emph_____
5.	Mesmerize or put in a trance	hypno_____
6.	Publicize widely	adver_____
7.	Give the body a good workout	exer_____
8.	Make a careful study of	ana_____
9.	Take away power of movement	para_____
10.	Come to know or conceive as real	real_____
11.	Have a feeling of sympathy for	sympa_____

ANSWERS TO SELF-TEST

1. apologize
2. authorize
3. baptize
4. emphasize
5. hypnotize
6. advertise

7. exercise
8. analyze
9. paralyze
10. realize
11. sympathize

CHAPTER 15

Grievous Sins, Mischievous Pranks, and Heinous Crimes

The title of this chapter might be a bit dramatic but it illustrates a common error in the spelling of the key words. Those three words are generally misspelled GRIEVIOUS, MISCHIEVIOUS, and HEINIOUS. The i before –ous results from the pressure of other examples (such as DUBIOUS, INGENIOUS, LUXURIOUS, and PREVIOUS).

Five word endings are often confused: –ious, –eous, –ous, –ius, and –us. The lists of words ending in –ious and –ous are just about equally long, and they account for most of the words dealt with in this chapter. The –ius list actually contains only one common word (GENIUS) although there are a few specialized words in this category. The –us words are all nouns, while the –ious, –eous, and –ous words are all adjectives.

1. Here are the most common words ending in just –us:

bonus	consensus	impetus
campus	cumulus	mucus*
calculus	focus	nimbus
caucus	genus	onus
census	hiatus	opus
circus	hippopotamus	prospectus
cirrus	ignoramus	stratus
citrus		

---

*Note that the adjective form is MUCOUS. Compare the spellings.

Supply the words that fit the following definitions.

(a) Extra money given as a reward for service   bon_____

(b) Site of college buildings   cam_____

(c) Branch of higher mathematics   calc_____

(d) Thick-skinned, water-loving animal   hipp_____

(e) Entertainment for children of all ages   circ_____

(f) Population count   cens_____

(g) Acid fruit such as lemons and oranges   citr_____

- - - - - - - - - - - - - - - -

    (a) bonus; (b) campus; (c) calculus; (d) hippopotamus; (e) circus;
(f) census; (g) citrus

2. Here are the most common words ending in –ious:

ambitious	furious	notorious
anxious	gracious	nutritious
auspicious	gregarious	oblivious
avaricious	harmonious	obnoxious
bilious	hilarious	obsequious
capricious	ignominious	officious
cautious	illustrious	ostentatious
ceremonious	impervious	parsimonious
conscientious	infectious	penurious
conscious	ingenious*	perspicacious
contagious	judicious	pious**
copious	laborious	precarious
curious	lascivious	precious
delicious	licentious	precocious
devious	luscious	pretentious
dubious	luxurious	previous
egregious	malicious	pugnacious
facetious	melodious	rapacious
fastidious	meritorious	religious
ferocious	mysterious	repetitious
fictitious	nefarious	sacrilegious***

*Note that another word, INGENUOUS, is often confused with this one.
**This word really belongs in the –ous list, because the i is not part of
the ending.
***Because of its association with things RELIGIOUS, this word is often
mispronounced and therefore misspelled.

sagacious	surreptitious	vicarious
salacious	suspicious	vicious
sanctimonious	tedious	victorious
specious	tenacious	vivacious
spurious	various	voracious

Circle each misspelled word below and write the correct spelling in the space beside it.

(a) grievious _____   (f) pius   _____

(b) fictitous _____   (g) mischievous _____

(c) notorious _____   (h) sacreligious _____

(d) heinous   _____   (i) previous   _____

(e) curious   _____   (j) anxious   _____

- - - - - - - - - - - - - -

(a) grievous; (b) fictitious; (c) pious; (d) sacri<u>le</u>gious

Note: There is also a proper name PIUS, as in Pope Pius XII.

3. The -eous words probably cause the most trouble among the words covered in this chapter because they cannot be distinguished from –ious words by sound. Since there are only a few -eous words, study the following list carefully and assume that the other words with like-sounding endings are spelled with –ious.

beauteous	extemporaneous	instantaneous
bounteous	gaseous	outrageous
contemporaneous	gorgeous	piteous
courteous	hideous	plenteous
crustaceous	herbaceous	righteous*
curvaceous	heterogeneous	sebaceous
discourteous	homogeneous	spontaneous
erroneous	igneous	

_____

*Actually pronounced rī-́chus, but it has to go somewhere.

Circle each misspelled word below and write the correct spelling in the space beside it.

(a) pitious _____   (f) instantaneous _____

(b) courteous _____   (g) continueous _____

(c) hidious _____   (h) gaseous _____

(d) gorgeous _____   (i) erronious _____

(e) rightious _____   (j) outrageous _____

- - - - - - - - - - - - - - -

(a) piteous; (c) hideous; (e) righteous; (g) continuous; (i) erroneous

4. In addition to the three key words in the title of this chapter (GRIEVOUS, MISCHIEVOUS, and HEINOUS), another often-mispronounced (and therefore misspelled) key word will come to mind if you have a friend in the hospital who is being fed through a vein. That is INTRAVENOUS feeding. If you are used to saying that word as if it had an –ious ending and therefore spell it INTRAVENIOUS—or even INTRAVEINIOUS—change your ways!

Getting the ending right with the other -ous words is relatively easy. Here are the most common words ending in -ous:

amorous	fabulous	intravenous
amorphous	famous	jealous
anonymous	fibrous	joyous
barbarous	fortuitous	lecherous
blasphemous	frivolous	libelous
boisterous	garrulous	ludicrous
callous	generous	luminous
cantankerous	glamorous	lustrous
clamorous	grievous	marvelous
conspicuous	hazardous	meticulous
contemptuous	heinous	miraculous
continuous	horrendous	mischievous
dangerous	humorous	momentous
desirous	impetuous	monotonous
dexterous	incestuous	monstrous
diaphanous	incongruous*	mucous
disastrous	ingenuous	multitudinous
enormous	innocuous	murderous

*Note the u before the ending. Some of the other words (CONSPICUOUS, IMPETUOUS) also have a u before the ending, but it is sounded clearly and not likely to be omitted in such words.

nebulous	proliferous	tempestuous
nervous	promiscuous	tenuous
numerous	querulous	timorous
obstreperous	raucous	tortuous
odoriferous	ravenous	torturous
ominous	ridiculous	treacherous
onerous	scandalous	tremendous
perilous	scrupulous	tremulous
pompous	scurrilous	tumultuous
ponderous	sinuous	ubiquitous
populous	strenuous	unanimous
porous	stupendous	venomous
precipitous	sumptuous	virtuous
preposterous	superfluous*	zealous
presumptuous	synonymous	

Circle each misspelled word below and write the correct spelling in the space beside it.

(a) barbarious _____

(b) boisterous _____

(c) desireous _____

(d) grievious _____

(e) humorous _____

(f) joious _____

(g) mischievious _____

(h) murderous _____

(i) nervious _____

(j) ridiculous _____

(k) stupendious _____

(l) treacherous _____

(m) tremendous _____

(n) virtuous _____

– – – – – – – – – – – – – –

(a) barbarous; (c) desirous; (d) grievous; (f) joyous; (g) mischievous; (i) nervous; (k) stupendous

*Not SUPERFULOUS.

SELF-TEST

The following list contains examples of all the various endings studied in this chapter. Circle each misspelled word and write the correct spelling in the space beside it.

1. courtious	_____	13. plentious	_____
2. ceremonious	_____	14. officious	_____
3. ferocius	_____	15. varius	_____
4. dubious	_____	16. copeous	_____
5. synchronous	_____	17. spontaneous	_____
6. erroneous	_____	18. gaseous	_____
7. pitious	_____	19. calculus	_____
8. hilarious	_____	20. dangerous	_____
9. grievous	_____	21. lustrious	_____
10. intraveinous	_____	22. disastrous	_____
11. genius	_____	23. fortuitious	_____
12. sacreligious	_____	24. perilous	_____

ANSWERS TO SELF-TEST

1. courteous	13. plenteous
3. ferocious	15. various
7. piteous	16. copious
10. intravenous	21. lustrous
12. sacrilegious	23. fortuitous

CHAPTER 16

Make the Connection Between *-sion* and *-tion*

The English spell that title word CONNEXION. In America the -xion ending is almost unheard of except in CRUCIFIXION and in the name of a detergent.

Both -sion and -tion are pronounced more or less like "shun," so sound is no help in spelling words with these endings. Since countless nouns are created by adding one of these endings to a verb, there is a lot of room for error. Most of these errors result when -sion words are misspelled with the -tion ending. (For some reason, people don't usually misspell the -tion words, or if they do, they get the endings right!) Some of these misspellings are: EXTENTION, EXPANTION, and COMPULTION. The correct spellings of these words are:

> extension   expansion   compulsion

Fortunately, there are some guidelines to help you remember when to write -sion rather than the more common -tion.

1. Study the following words and try to note a relationship between the form of the noun and the spelling of the basic word from which each was derived:

> extend, extension   expand, expansion
> pretend, pretension   condescend, condescension

If the basic word ends in -nd, the noun form probably ends in _____.

                                                      (-tion/-sion)

— — — — — — — — — — — — — —

   -sion

Note: But the noun form of INTEND is INTENTION.

2. Now study the following words:

persuade, persuasion	conclude, conclusion
invade, invasion	erode, erosion
deride, derision	provide, provision

If the basic word ends in –de, the noun form probably ends in _____.

(–sion/–tion)

– – – – – – – – – – – –

   –sion

3. Study the following sample words:

express, expression	discuss, discussion

If the basic word ends in –ss, the noun is formed by adding the ending

_____.

(–tion/–sion/–ion)

– – – – – – – – – – – –

   –ion

Note: If the ending were –sion, the noun form of EXPRESS would be EXPRESSSION!

4. Examine the spelling changes in the following words:

admit, admission	omit, omission
transmit, transmission	remit, remission

When the verb ends in –mit, the noun form ends in _____.

– – – – – – – – – – – –

   –mission

5. Study still another group of words:

compel, compulsion	repel, repulsion
expel, expulsion	propel, propulsion

When the verb ends in –pel, the noun form probably ends in –p_____.

– – – – – – – – – – – –

   –pulsion

6. Study the following words:

revert, reversion   convert, conversion
pervert, perversion   divert, diversion

When the verb ends in –vert, the noun form probably ends in –v_____.

– – – – – – – – – – – – – –

-version

7. Write the noun forms of the following verbs:

(a) ascend   _____   (f) propel   _____

(b) protrude _____   (g) invert   _____

(c) divide   _____   (h) exclude   _____

(d) compress _____   (i) persuade   _____

(e) transmit _____   (j) expand   _____

– – – – – – – – – – – – – –

(a) ascension; (b) protrusion; (c) division; (d) compression;
(e) transmission; (f) propulsion; (g) inversion; (h) exclusion;
(i) persuasion; (j) expansion

8. Study the following words:

act, action   restrict, restriction
construct, construction   correct, correction
concoct, concoction   connect, connection

When the verb ends in –ct, the noun is formed by adding the ending

_____.

(-sion/-tion/-ion)

– – – – – – – – – – – – – –

-ion

9. Study the following words:

propose, proposition   compose, composition

When artists' models pose, they are really working hard because they

have to hold the same _____ for many minutes.
                 (form of POSE)

– – – – – – – – – – – – –

position

10. Often <u>internal</u> letters of the original verb are changed when an ending is added to create the noun form:

retain, retention   redeem, redemption

discreet,* discretion   absorb, absorption

A significant part of the _____ of goods is accom-
(form of CONSUME)

plished through the _____ of trading stamps.
(form of REDEEM)

- - - - - - - - - - - - - -

 consumption, redemption

11. The great majority of –tion nouns are formed from verbs ending in –te. Some of these are:

distribute, distribution   create, creation

promote, promotion   dilute, dilution

Write the –ion forms of the following verbs:

(a) dissipate _____ (c) rotate _____

(b) contribute _____ (d) devote _____

- - - - - - - - - - - - - -

 (a) dissipation; (b) contribution; (c) rotation; (d) devotion

12. In many cases, the ending of the noun form might be –ation, not –tion, but this presents no problem because the first vowel of the ending is clearly heard:

present, presentation   retard, retardation

condemn, condemnation   commute, commutation

Write the noun forms of the following verbs:

(a) orient _____ (c) solicit _____

(b) damn _____ (d) console _____

- - - - - - - - - - - - - -

 (a) orientation; (b) damnation; (c) solicitation; (d) consolation

_____

*DISCREET is one of the few adjectives that has a noun form ending in –ion rather than in –sion or –tion.

13. Be especially careful of changes within the original verb when the noun ending is -ation:

pronounce, pronunciation	proclaim, proclamation
explain, explanation	repair, reparation

Using the examples as a guide, write the noun forms of the following verbs:

(a) denounce _____

(b) reclaim _____

— — — — — — — — — — — — — —

   (a) denunciation; (b) reclamation

SELF-TEST

Write the noun form of each of the following verbs:

1.	extend	_____	11.	instruct	_____
2.	explode	_____	12.	react	_____
3.	intend	_____	13.	oppose	_____
4.	deprive	_____	14.	dissuade	_____
5.	suppress	_____	15.	retain	_____
6.	omit	_____	16.	consume	_____
7.	compel	_____	17.	solicit	_____
8.	convert	_____	18.	exhibit	_____
9.	converse	_____	19.	pollute	_____
10.	condescend	_____	20.	pronounce	_____

ANSWERS TO SELF-TEST

1. extension
2. explosion
3. intention
4. deprivation
5. suppression
6. omission
7. compulsion
8. conversion
9. conversation
10. condescension
11. instruction
12. reaction
13. opposition
14. dissuasion
15. retention
16. consumption
17. solicitation
18. exhibition
19. pollution
20. pronunciation

CHAPTER 17

The Ant and the Ent

The ant needs no introduction, and the ent is a tree-person from the Tolkien books. Both are easy to spell. Not so the many words ending in these letters.

There are no reliable guidelines to help you sort out these words so that you know when to end with -ant and when with -ent because the endings are not clearly distinguished in speech. The word lists given later in the chapter will help. For the most part, these are actually pairs of words (for example, DECADENT and DECADENCE, or FRAGRANT and FRAGRANCE). In all cases, however, if you spell one form with a (or e), you follow the same rule for the other form.

1. Fill in the blanks:

important	import__nce
evid__nt	evidence
frequent	frequ__ncy

– – – – – – – – – – – – – – –

importance, evident, frequency

2. There is an additional complication in the -ance or -ence form: Is that letter before the silent e an s or a c? That problem can be solved right now, and very simply. Here are the -se words; all the other common ones end in -ce:

defense	offense	suspense
expense	pretense	tense
incense	recompense	expanse
license	sense	

One word was taken out of alphabetical order to make a point. EXPANSE also ends in -se, but it is the only common word that ends in -anse rather than -ense.

Write the -nce/-nse forms of the following words:

(a) pretend _____   (d) expand _____

(b) defend _____   (e) suspend _____

(c) offend _____   (f) expend _____

- - - - - - - - - - - - - - -

(a) pretense; (b) defense; (c) offense; (d) expanse; (e) suspense; (f) expense

Note: All six verbs in this frame end in -nd. This is an additional clue in remembering more than half the -nse words.

The following list includes the main words ending in -ant, -ent, -ance, -ence, -ancy, and -ency. To save space, just one form of most words is given. The choice of form is arbitrary, although the more common form is usually shown. Read the list carefully and check off any words you normally misspell and any words with endings that surprise you.

abeyance	assurance	convalescence
abhorrence	attendance	convenience
absence	audience	conversant
absorbent	belligerent	conveyance
abstinence	brilliant	correspondence
abundance		countenance
accountant	circumference	crescent
acquaintance	circumstance	currant
adjacent	clairvoyance	current
admittance	clearance	decadence
adolescence	coexistence	defendant
affluence	coherence	deference
allegiance	coincidence	defiance
alliance	combatant	deficient
allowance	competence	delinquent
ambulance	complacent	dependence
ancient	compliance	descendant
annoyance	concurrence	despondent
antecedent	condolence	deterrent
apparent	confidence	deviant
appearance	consequence	different
appliance	consistent	diligence
applicant	constituent	disappearance
arrogance	consultant	discordant
assistance	contrivance	

discrepant
disinfectant
distance
disturbance
divergence
dominance
dormant

effervescent
efficiency
efficient
elegant
eloquence
emigrant
encumbrance
endurance
enhance
entrance
equivalent
errant
essence
evidence
excellence
exorbitant
expectant
experience
extravagance

fancy
fence
finance
flippant
fluent
fluorescent
forbearance
fragrant
fraudulent
frequency
frequent

gallant
gallivant
grievance
guidance

hindrance

ignorance
imbalance
imminent
impatient
impertinence
importance
impotent
imprudent
incandescent
incessant
incidence
incipient
inclement
incoherent
incompetent
incumbent
independent
indignant
indolent
indulgence
infancy
infant
inference
influence
infrequent
ingredient
inhabitant
inherent
inheritance
innocence
insignificant
insistent
instance
intelligent
intolerant
iridescent
irrelevant
irreverent
irritant
itinerant

jubilant

latent
lieutenant

luminescent
luxuriant

magnificence
maintenance
malevolent
malfeasance
malignant
mendicant
merchant
migrant

nascent
necromancy
negligence
nonchalant
nuance

obedient
obeisance
obsolescent
occupant
occurrence
omnipotent
opalescent
opponent
opulence
ordinance
ordnance

pageant
parlance
participant
patience
penance
penchant
pendant[*]
pendent[*]
penitence
pennant
performance
permanence
perseverance
persistent
pertinent
pestilence

---

[*]PENDANT, ornament; PENDENT, hanging

petulant
pheasant
pleasant
pliant
poignant
potent
precedence
predominant
pre-eminence
preference
presence
prevalence
proficient
prominence
protuberance
providence
pursuant
pubescent
putrescent

quiescent
quotient

radiance
rampant
recalcitrant
recent
recipient
reconnaissance
recurrence
redundant
reference
relevant
reliance
reluctant

remembrance
reminiscent
remittance
remittent
remnant
remonstrance
repellent
repentance
repugnant
resemblance
resistance
resonant
resplendent
respondent
restaurant
resultant
resurgent
reticence
reverent
riddance

salient
science
semblance
sentence
sentient
sequence
severance
significance
solvent
stimulant
strident
stringent
submergence

subsequent
subservient
subsistence
substance
sufficient
surveillance
sustenance
sycophant

talent
tangent
temperance
tenant
tolerance
transcendent
transference
transient
translucent
transparent
triumphant
truant
truculence
tumescent
turbulence

vacant
valance*
valence*
valiant
variance
verdant
vibrant
vigilance
violence

3. Careful study of the foregoing list will yield a bonus. There are a number of words in which the combination of sc (pronounced s) precedes the ending. With the exception of CRESCENT, they all have two forms (ADOLESCENT, ADOLESCENCE), and they all end in -scent/-scence (which means "becoming"). On the following page, they are listed in a group by themselves.

---

*VALANCE, drapery; VALENCE, chemistry

adolescent	iridescent	pubescent
convalescent	luminescent	putrescent
crescent	nascent	quiescent
effervescent	obsolescent	reminiscent
fluorescent	opalescent	tumescent
incandescent		

Please note traps in three words. In FLUORESCENT, u comes before o.
There is only one r in IRIDESCENT. The vowel before the ending in
REMINISCENT is i.

When Edison invented the incand_____light bulb, he could hardly

have foreseen the widespread use of the fl_____ tube, more

sophisticated lumin_____ devices, and the exotic ir_____
displays of more modern times.

- - - - - - - - - - - - - -

incandescent, fluorescent, luminescent, iridescent

SELF-TEST

1. Circle each misspelled word below and write the correct spelling in the space beside it.

(a) abstinence   _____

(b) admittanse   _____

(c) allegiance   _____

(d) apparant   _____

(e) assistence   _____

(f) coherense   _____

(g) correspondance   _____

(h) deficient   _____

(i) discrepency   _____

(j) fluorescant   _____

(k) malignent   _____

(l) occurrance   _____

(m) recent   _____

(n) reconnaissance   _____

(o) recurrence   _____

(p) reminisent   _____

(q) resplendant   _____

(r) sequence   _____

(s) subsequant   _____

(t) transference   _____

(u) transient   _____

(v) translucant   _____

(w) turbulance   _____

(x) vacant   _____

(y) valiant   _____

(z) vigilance   _____

2. Fill in the blanks in these three columns. In some cases, you will have a choice of correct words.

Noun	Verb	Adjective
abhorrence	abhor	abhorrent
alliance	ally	allied
(a)_____	acquaint	acquainted
complacency	(none)	(f)_____
(b)_____	(none)	current
(c)_____	differ	(g)_____
(d)_____	defy	(h)_____
(e)_____	convalesce	(i)_____

ANSWERS TO SELF-TEST

1. (b) admittance
   (d) apparent
   (e) assistance
   (f) coherence
   (g) correspondence
   (i) discrepancy
   (j) fluorescent

   (k) malignant
   (l) occurrence
   (p) reminiscent
   (s) subsequent
   (v) translucent
   (w) turbulence

2. (a) acquaintance
   (b) currency or current
   (c) difference
   (d) defiance
   (e) convalescence

   (f) complacent
   (g) different
   (h) defiant
   (i) convalescent

CHAPTER 18

Identify *-ify* and *-efy*

Most words ending in –ify or –efy are easy. The ending is –ify as in the following examples:

identify	pacify	beautify
stultify	magnify	certify
mystify	horrify	

The other forms related to these words are equally easy. Consider IDENTIFIED, IDENTIFICATION; MAGNIFIED, MAGNIFICATION; CERTIFIED, CERTIFICATION, CERTIFICATE.

1. Fill in the blanks:

stultify	stultified	stultification
	pacified	
_____	_____	beautification

– – – – – – – – – – – – – – –

   pacify, pacification; beautify, beautified

2. The handful of words with the –efy ending are not as commonly used (which might be the reason they have retained the lesser-known ending). The noun forms are also different, but the difference is <u>regular</u>, which makes life simple.

   Following the pattern of the sample words, fill in the blanks:

liquefy	liquefaction
putrefy	putrefaction
rarefy	_____
_____	stupefaction

_ _ _ _ _ _ _ _ _ _ _ _ _ _

rarefaction, stupefy

3. If the verb ends with -efy, the noun ends with _____.

_ _ _ _ _ _ _ _ _ _ _ _ _ _

-efaction

Note that SATISFY, whose noun form is SATISFACTION, does not fit either category. The reason for the different form of the noun goes all the way back to Latin and is beyond the scope of this book.

SELF-TEST

Circle each misspelled word below and write the correct spelling beside it.

1.	mystefy	_____	6.	certification	_____
2.	identify	_____	7.	putrify	_____
3.	beautification	_____	8.	stupefy	_____
4.	liquify	_____	9.	magnefication	_____
5.	rarefaction	_____	10.	pacify	_____

ANSWERS TO SELF-TEST

1. mystify   7. putrefy
4. liquefy   9. magnification

CHAPTER 19

The Butcher, the Actor, and the Candlestick Maker

The overwhelming majority of doers and shakers, movers and makers are identified as to occupation by words that end in -er. But there are other endings. Some of these are -or, -eer, -ier, and (in the heady atmosphere of French loan words) -eur, and -euse.

1. If the occupation has been with us for a long, long time, the ending is very likely to be -er (but note DOCTOR, ACTOR, and CONQUEROR).

Trying to work out rules is a tricky business, but generally speaking, if a person works with things (bread, meat, candles) or is in a building trade (CARPENTER, PAINTER, PLUMBER), his occupation is probably spelled with -er. If a person deals in intangibles or services rather than goods, his occupation is probably spelled with -or.

Here are several examples of the -or occupations:

supervisor	conqueror	bettor
mortgagor	editor	donor
competitor	monitor	doctor
professor	counselor	cantor
conductor	councilor	actor
collector	contractor	lessor
instructor	director	

Note that a member of a city COUNCIL is a COUNCILOR, while one who gives COUNSEL is a COUNSELOR.

The young man worked as a house painter, carp_____,

apprentice plum_____, and supervi_____ of a construction gang while
he tried to establish himself as a writer. Later he had a part-time job

as an instruc_____ at a junior college, where a friendly profess_____

read his unpublished novel and introduced him to the edi_____ of a large
publishing firm. Last year he won a Pulitizer prize.

— — — — — — — — — — — — — — —

carpenter, plumber, supervisor, instructor, professor, editor

2. <u>Things</u> that do something are generally spelled with -or. These include words like INDICATOR, PERCOLATOR, MOTOR, GENERATOR,
and ALTERNATOR (but compare COMPUTER and PROPELLER).

An electrician on the job might have to repair a small mot_____,

a generat_____, or even the control wiring to a ship's propell_____,

but he would not be expected to troubleshoot a comput_____. When he
gets home, he might have to check the television or the electric perco-

lat_____.

— — — — — — — — — — — — — — —

motor, generator, propeller, computer, percolator

3. The -eer occupations give no trouble, because the ending is plainly
heard. However, note two common exceptions (both having to do with
money): FINANCIER and CASHIER.

The businessman got his start as an honest auction_____, but the

war brought him temptation as a black market profit_____. Although

his past was tainted by association with confidence men and racket_____,

he finally became a stock broker and liked to be thought of as a financ_____.

— — — — — — — — — — — — — — —

auctioneer, profiteer, racketeers, financier

4. Several occupations are French loan words. One who excels in story-telling is a RACONTEUR. One knowledgeable in a special subject, such as fine wines, is a CONNOISSEUR. A singer of sultry songs in the manner of Edith Piaf is a CHANTEUSE (note the feminine ending). And one who pounds and pummels tired and flabby muscles is a MASSEUR (masculine) or a MASSEUSE (feminine). Then there is the gentleman who risks his capital in the hope of making a profit—the ENTREPRENEUR. If he is successful, he might feel it worthwhile to hire a CHAUFFEUR.

Fill in the blanks:

(a) A teller of entertaining tales is a _____ .

(b) An expert in Swedish massage is a _____ if he is a

man and a _____ if she is a woman.

(c) Many a taxicab driver hopes to someday become a _____

for a wealthy employer.

- - - - - - - - - - - - - -

(a) raconteur; (b) masseur, masseuse; (c) chauffeur

SELF-TEST

Supply the word ending in r that is related to each of the following words or phrases:

1.	medicine	_____	11.	mortgage _____
2.	acting	_____	12.	counsel _____
3.	plumbing	_____	13.	direction _____
4.	driving	ch_____	14.	massage _____
5.	computation	_____	15.	profit p_____
6.	propel	_____	16.	auction _____
7.	indicate	_____	17.	finance _____
8.	supervise	_____	18.	conquer _____
9.	fine wines	c_____	19.	coffee pot _____
10.	instruction	_____	20.	capital en_____

ANSWERS TO SELF-TEST

1.	doctor		11.	mortgagor
2.	actor		12.	counselor
3.	plumber		13.	director
4.	chauffeur		14.	masseur
5.	computer		15.	profiteer
6.	propeller		16.	auctioneer
7.	indicator		17.	financier
8.	supervisor		18.	conqueror
9.	connoisseur		19.	percolator
10.	instructor		20.	entrepreneur

CHAPTER 20

Exceed Your Goal and Proceed to Succeed

Almost everyone has trouble with the group of words in which the ending always sounds like "seed" but is spelled any one of three different ways: -cede, -ceed, -sede. A little work with memorizing (just as you had to learn the multiplication tables) will clear up this problem. Here are the three lists of words:

accede	exceed	supersede
concede	proceed	
intercede	succeed	
precede		
recede		
secede		

1. The words ending in -cede all come from the Latin <u>cedere</u>, which means to go, to move, or to yield. In addition to the words in which -cede is an ending, there is the basic word CEDE, which means to yield. A country might CEDE some of its territory to another country, for example.

The following "definitions" are not exact in English, since shades of meaning change somewhat over the years, but here are the -cede words again in terms of their etymology, or history:

accede: go toward (He must ACCEDE to our proposal.)

concede: go with (Will you CONCEDE that I am right?)

intercede: go between (He is going to INTERCEDE for us.)

precede: go before (An investigation must PRECEDE a
final decision.)

recede: go back (The flood waters have begun to RECEDE.)

secede: move aside (The South tried to SECEDE from the
Union.)

During the years pre_____ the outbreak of war, a num-
               (going before)

ber of smaller nations tried to inter_____ , offering their
                                    (go between)

good offices to help settle the dispute, but neither superpower would

con_____ that the other's complaints had merit.
        (acknowledge)

— — — — — — — — — — — — —

   preceding, intercede, concede

2. The next three words are all used frequently, and words that are
most often used in conversation are also the ones that are most likely to
undergo a change in spelling as time goes by. Therefore, it should be
no surprise that these three come from the same Latin verb as the preceding group:

        exceed: go beyond (He is prone to EXCEED his authority.)

        proceed: go forward (Let us PROCEED with the business
                  at hand.)

        succeed: go along (You are bound to SUCCEED if you don't
                  give up.)

The noun forms EXCESS and SUCCESS present no problem in spelling
because the ending is clearly heard in speech, but the noun form of PRO-
CEED is often misspelled PROCEEDURE. Be sure to drop one e and
spell it PROCEDURE.

    The chemist ex_____ all expectations in developing a
                  (went beyond)

low-cost pro_____ure that would suc_____ in isolating the
          (method)   (be successful)
rare element under field conditions.

— — — — — — — — — — — — —

   exceeded, procedure, succeed

3. The final word to be considered in this chapter is almost universally
misspelled because of the understandable tendency to lump it with the
-cede words. SUPERSEDE comes from the Latin sedere, which means
to sit. Thus, SUPERSEDE really means to sit above. It is the only
-sede word, and once you have read this you are not likely to misspell it
again.

The United Nations super_____ the League of Nations as a world forum after the end of World War II.

— — — — — — — — — — — — — —

superseded

Memorize the sentence that is the title of this chapter:

Exceed your goal and proceed to succeed.

When you have done that, you have solved the whole problem of –cede, –ceed, and –sede words since all the other words end in –cede, with the single exception of SUPERSEDE.

SELF-TEST

1. Write the only three words that end in –ceed:

(a) _____

(b) _____

(c) _____

2. What is the only word in English that ends in –sede? _____

_____

3. A bad storm is often pre_____ by a sudden drop in atmos-
pheric pressure. Afterwards, the community must pro_____
to repair the damage and treat the injured.

ANSWERS TO SELF-TEST

1. (a) exceed
   (b) proceed
   (c) succeed

2. supersede

3. preceded, proceed

CHAPTER 21

The Reckoning

Finally we come to the time of reckoning. This chapter provides you with the opportunity to see how well <u>we</u> have done—you and I. My purpose in writing this book was to give you some guidelines and insights into the structures of words with the hope that you would be able to use the information to accomplish <u>your</u> purpose, which was to improve your spelling.

This final chapter is essentially an examination by which you may test your understanding of the principles set forth in the book. Some of the words may be new, but they all follow guidelines you have studied or are specifically noted exceptions. There is no passing or failing grade. You will be the judge of your own performance.

It is doubtful that you will ever again see such a long answer section for a 100-word examination. The reason is simply that there will be new learning in this chapter, as in all the others. All words in the answer section are followed by one or more numbers in parentheses that represent chapter references. If you miss a word, refer to the appropriate chapters to review the material that will help you avoid misspelling that word in the future. If you find yourself frequently referring to the same chapter, it would be wise to reword that entire chapter.

Many of the words in the answer section are followed by notes or spelling hints to help you fix the proper spelling firmly in your mind. Often there are references to other words to keep you from misspelling related words that follow a slightly different pattern.

Keep working on the 100 words in the examination until you are satisfied that you can spell them <u>all</u> correctly. When you can do so, you can be pretty sure that you have the basic rules of spelling clear in your mind, and you will find that you will also be able to spell a great many other words correctly.

The fact that you can <u>recognize</u> a correctly spelled word is no assurance that you could have spelled that word correctly in the first place. Thus, the questions are designed so that you write the word yourself from the information given in the question. (Sometimes a few letters of the word might be provided, but this is only to make sure you know which word is intended; it is not a crutch to help you spell the word.)

Take all the time you need to take the test. Do not rush through the answers. The number of words you get right is of secondary importance. The primary goal is a thorough understanding of the structure of written English words.

FINAL SELF-TEST

Each of the following questions requires you to fill in the blank with a certain word. Various means are used to make sure you identify the word asked for. In some cases, modified dictionary pronunciation is given.

1. Rickets often occurs when the diet is _____ in vitamin D. (dē fĭsh′ ĕnt)

2. In some families, three subjects never discussed at dinner are sex, religion, and p_____. (pŏl′ ĭ tĭks)

3. He paid an extremely high rent for the _____ apartment. (form of LUXURY)

4. His statements were dismissed as sheer _____. (hĭ pŏk′ rĭ sĭ)

5. The Internal Revenue Service ruled that the expense was not a _____ item. (adjective form of DEDUCTION)

6. To disable or destroy the ability to move is to par_____.

7. The plural of CRISIS is _____.

8. Many words are misspelled because of poor _____ion. (form of PRONOUNCE)

9. Your can_____ check can serve as a receipt. (form of CANCEL)

10. The birth of quintuplets is a rare oc_____. (form of OCCUR)

11. Blackstone captivated audiences with extr_____ feats of magic. (highly unusual, remarkable)

12. The chemistry student had to wait for two hours for the solution to cry_____. (form CRYSTALS)

13. The state of being LONELY is l_____.

14. His statements were regarded as not only profane and irreverent but sacr_____ous.

15. To be in excess of what is sufficient is to be superf_____s.

16. His book was scholarly, but the introduction omitted _____ of several important sources. (ăk nŏl'ĕj mĕnt)

17. The surgeon ordered intra_____ feeding of the patient for forty-eight hours after the operation. (ĭn tră vē'nŭs)

18. The robber's brother-in-law was arrested as an _____ after the fact. (ăk sĕs'ō rĭ)

19. The plural of COURT-MARTIAL is _____.

20. He was fond of pointing out that it was not an _____ but a discussion. (form of ARGUE)

21. The p_____ of a boat or ship is sometimes called a screw. (form of PROPEL)

22. The contraction for IT IS is _____.

23. Every soldier in the unit received i_____ in survival techniques. (form of INSTRUCT)

24. The blonde show girl was often described as c_____. (form of CURVE as applied to female figure)

25. It is imp_____ble to burn water.

26. No one could believe he was guilty of the _____ crime.
(hā′nŭs)

27. Reading is a b_____ skill that must be learned early.
(form of BASE)

28. A complimentary close of many business letters is, "Yours
t_____."

29. Prompt attention to emergency procedures took p_____
over other matters. (form of PRECEDE)

30. He quickly learned how to _____ his feelings. (dĭs gīz′)

31. The feminine word corresponding to NEPHEW is _____.

32. Until she turned on the lights and was startled by the shouted greet-
ings, she had no hint of the sur_____ birthday party.

33. Construction engineers have to know a lot about stress and
_____. (strān)

34. The plural of KNIFE is _____.

35. According to the Declaration of Independence, "All men are
_____ equal."

36. The goal was to in_____ate everyone in the community
against smallpox. (to inject an immunizing serum)

37. After Pearl Harbor, the nation swiftly mobilized for _____.
(form of DEFEND)

38. The huge book had nine ap_____s at the back.
(ă pĕn′ dĭk sĕz)

39. Always include pickles in the PICNIC basket when the family goes
pic_____ing.

40. The nation was scandalized by the king's mar_____ to a
commoner. (form of MARRY)

41. He obtained a driver's li_____ when he was sixteen years
old.

42. The plural of 7 is _____.

43. "The Hatfields and the Coys" is a ballad about a famous _____.
(fūd)

44. The evidence, although only circumstantial, was extremely
com_____ing. (form of COMPEL)

45. A place where petroleum is REFINED is called a r_____y.

46. One who conducts an AUCTION is called an a_____.

47. The community had to raise property taxes to pay for the new
housing devel_____.

48. Fraud is an attempt to de_____ the victim. (verb form of
DECEPTION)

49. Long tubes are used in fl_____nt lighting.

50. A microscope is used to mag_____ the images of very small
objects.

51. Her house was always im_____. (ĭ măk′ ū lĭt)

52. After a siege of two weeks, the invaders were able to _____ the fortress. (sēz)

53. The candidate was always ac_____ by two bodyguards. (ă kŭm′ pă nĭd)

54. The plural of CALF is _____.

55. Public drunk_____ is a misdemeanor in many states. (intoxication)

56. His supervisor refused to rec_____nd him for a promotion.

57. The fishing village was located on a tribu_____ of the Mississippi River. (trĭb′ ū tĕr ĭ)

58. They were given two seats on the _____. (sounds like "I'll")

59. The young mother knew she would di_____oint her children if she did not find a way to give them a happy Christmas.

60. The only gate to the launch area was locked, and there was no _____ without proper authority. (ăd mĭt ăns)

61. The d_____ of the film won an Academy Award. (one who DIRECTS)

62. The cal_____ is a branch of higher mathematics. (kăl kū lŭs)

63. The judge warned the defendant that his behavior might lead to his exp_____ion from the courtroom. (form of EXPEL)

64. The Chairman appointed a three-man com_____ to investigate the project. (kŏ mǐt′ǐ)

65. The praying mantis is, in both color and shape, a striking example of protective m_____ry. (form of MIMIC)

66. The length, breadth, and h_____ of the structure were carefully measured. (related to HIGH)

67. The bewildered prisoner seemed hardly con_____ of his surroundings. (kŏn′shŭs)

68. He was _____ to discover that the joke was on him. (shă grind′)

69. He couldn't shake the p_____ cold. (form of PERSIST)

70. Her own welfare was of only sec_____ importance. (sĕk′ŏn dĕr ǐ)

71. To become liquid is to liq_____. (lĭk′wē fī)

72. Lady Bird Johnson was noted as a leader of the beaut_____tion program. (form of BEAUTY)

73. Edgar Allan Poe wrote strange, and sometimes _____, stories. (wērd)

74. The newspaper article was filled with er_____s statements. (from ERROR)

75. The plural of HERO is _____.

76. She passed the time on her daily bus ride with knitting and embroi_____.

77. Impatient with excuses and beating around the bush, he demanded a def_____ answer.

78. To make an APOLOGY is to ap_____.

79. The consequences of the act were not pre_____le. (form of PREDICT)

80. The company had a large budget to adver_____ its product on radio and television.

81. The efforts of the Red Cross bene_____ both sides in the war. (past tense of BENEFIT)

82. The parade was arranged so the U.S. Navy Band would pre_____ local marching units. (prē sed′)

83. Even the best-behaved children are sometimes m_____s. (form of MISCHIEF)

84. The plural of phenomenon is _____.

85. The new remedy was expected to _____ all medicines currently used. (sū pĕr sed′)

86. The more common plural of FOCUS is _____. (The less common plural is FOCI.)

87. The Four Hundred represent the cream of high soc_____. (sō sī′ĕ tĭ)

88. "If at first you don't s_____, try, try again."

89. Most Americans demonstrate a p_____ for steak over hamburger. (form of PREFER)

90. The possessive of WOMEN is _____.

91. One adjective form of PITY is pit_____ s.

92. The plural of M.D. is _____.

93. The opposite of WARMLY is coo_____.

94. His work required the wisdom of Solomon and the _____

of Job. (pā′shĕns)

95. The stage glowed with shifting, _____ colors.

(ĭr ĭ dĕs ĕnt)

96. The telegram began, "We _____ to inform you..." (are

sorry)

97. For centuries the Moslems were zealous in bringing about the

con_____ of new peoples to Islam. (form of CONVERT)

98. The plural of TARIFF is _____.

99. When you pay cash for a large purchase, be sure to get a

re_____. (rē sēt′)

100. When the pianist broke his hands, he lost his means of

l_____. (līv lĭ hood)

ANSWERS TO FINAL SELF-TEST

The numbers after the key words are principal chapter references.

1. deficient (8, 9, 11, 17). Also, PROFICIENT; but note EFFICIENT, SUFFICIENT.

2. politics (4). Other forms are POLITIC, POLITICKER, POLITICKING.

3. luxurious (5, 15). Note that y becomes i.

4. hypocrisy (4, 11). Hypo- means "under," while hyper- means "excessive." Compare HYPOCRITICAL and HYPERCRITICAL. Other words with the -sy ending are ECSTASY, HERESY, and IDIOSYNCRASY.

5. deductible (11, 13). Also DESTRUCTIBLE; but compare RETRACTABLE.

6. paralyze (14). But note PARALYSIS. Other -yze words are ANALYZE, CATALYZE, ELECTROLYZE, PSYCHOANALYZE.

7. crises (6). The singular is CRISIS. Note also BASIS, BASES; THESIS, THESES; DIAGNOSIS, DIAGNOSES; NEUROSIS, NEUROSES; PSYCHOSIS, PSYCHOSES.

8. pronunciation (16). Compare ANNUNCIATION, DENUNCIATION; don't be misled by ANNOUNCE, DENOUNCE, PRONOUNCE.

9. canceled (3). But note CANCELLATION.

10. occurrence (3, 17). Double c and double r. If something happens again, it is a RECURRENCE, not a RE-OCCURRENCE.

11. extraordinary (11, 12). Think of EXTRA + ORDINARY, but don't pronounce it that way!

12. crystallize (3, 14). Note the double l.

13. loneliness (2, 5). Remember that y becomes i in such words.

14. sacrilegious (15). Think of SACRILEGIOUS as the opposite of RELIGIOUS, and reverse the vowels also.

15. superfluous (11, 15). Note the u before -ous.

16. acknowledgment (2, 11). Drop the final e before most endings, as in ACKNOWLEDGING, JUDGMENT, but retain final e in KNOWLEDGEABLE.

17. intravenous (11, 15). Don't be misled by the fact that the word is related to VEIN.

18. accessory (11). Note that both c's are pronounced.

19. courts-martial (6). The key word of a compound takes the plural.

20. argument (2). Drop the final e before -ment in this word. Also note ARGUING.

21. propeller (3, 19). Note the -er ending, but compare ALTERNATOR, MOTOR, ROTOR, INDICATOR, PERCOLATOR.

22. it's (10). But the possessive is ITS.

23. instruction (16). Words that end in -ct, such as CONSTRUCT, RE-ACT, and AFFLICT, acutally have the ending -ion in the noun form.

24. curvaceous (9, 15). Note also HERBACEOUS, CRUSTACEOUS.

25. impossible (13). The ending -ible usually follows ss, as in ACCES-SIBLE, ADMISSIBLE, EXPRESSIBLE; but note PASSABLE, IMPASS-ABLE.

26. heinous (8, 15). Did you remember this one from the title of Chapter 15?

27. basic (2). Remember to drop final e before an ending that starts with a vowel.

28. truly (2). Drop the silent e in TRULY, DULY, and UNRULY.

29. precedence (17, 20). Note PRECEDE, RECEDE; but EXCEED, PROCEED, PROCEDURE, SUCCEEED, and SUPERSEDE.

30. disguise (4, 14). Many words have gu before i to indicate hard g. Also note -ise ending.

31. niece (7, 8). Long e is frequently indicated by ie.

32. surprise (14). But compare PRIZE.

33. strain (7). Long a is frequently indicated by ai.

34. knives (6). Note also the plurals LIVES, WIVES.

35. created (1, 2). The verb, CREATE, follows the basic silent e rule.

36. inoculate (11). Only one n. Don't be misled by words like INNO-VATE, INNOCENT, and INNOCUOUS.

37. defense (17). If the verb ends in -nd, the noun probably ends in -nse: DEFEND, DEFENSE; EXPAND, EXPANSE; RESPOND, RESPONSE.

38. appendixes (6). You're always safe if you use the more common plurals of words like INDEXES, MATRIXES, and APPENDIXES.

39. picnicking (4). Without the k, the word would sound like pick nice ing.

40. marriage (5). You don't hear the i in speech, but remember that it is there.

41. license (17). Note that it is –se, not –ce.

42. 7's (6). Always use 's for the plurals of numerals and letters.

43. feud (7). Another of those two-vowel combinations to indicate a long vowel sound.

44. compelling (3). The accent is on –pel, so double the l.

45. refinery (12). It includes the complete word REFINE and is a noun, so the ending is –ery.

46. auctioneer (19). And ENGINEER, PROFITEER, RACKETEER.

47. development (2). No final e in develop, but note envelop and envelope. There is no final e in envelop, which rhymes with develop.

48. deceive (8). Also PERCEIVE, RECEIVE, CONCEIVE.

49. fluorescent (17). Note that it is uo, not ou.

50. magnify (18). This word belongs with the majority: –ify, not –efy.

51. immaculate (11). The Latin is immaculatus, or "not spotted." Think of IM + MACULATE.

52. seize (8) Remember: NEITHER had LEISURE to SEIZE the WEIRD thing.

53. accompanied (5, 11). The prefix ac– occurs in many words, such as ACCOMMODATE, ACCESSORY, ACCEDE.

54. calves (6). Note also HALF, HALVES; LEAF, LEAVES.

55. drunkenness (3). Remember that double n!

56. recommend (11). Think of RE + COMMEND; no double c.

57. tributary (12). Often used as a noun, it's the adjective form of TRIBUTE, so spell it with –ary.

58. aisle (7). It's hard to forget the spelling of such an odd word!

59. disappoint (11). Only one s; think of DIS + APPOINT. Note also DISAPPROVE; but compare DISSIMILAR, DISSIPATE.

60. admittance (3, 11, 17). There is a double t in all such –mit words, such as OMITTING, TRASMITTER.

61. director (19). Also ACTOR, DOCTOR, EDITOR, PROFESSOR.

62. calculus (15). Also BONUS, CAMPUS, CALLUS, HIPPOPOTAMUS.

63. expulsion (16). EXPEL, EXPULSION; COMPEL, COMPULSION; PROPEL, PROPULSION; also REVULSION, CONVULSION.

64. committee (3, 11). Three double letters!

65. mimicry (4). No k in this word.

66. height (7, 8). Does not end with -th. Think of HEIGHT and WEIGHT.

67. conscious (9, 15). Think of sci in connection with mental processes: SCIENCE, CONSCIENCE, CONSCIONABLE.

68. chagrined (3, 9). One n. Remember this odd exception?

69. persistent (17). Also EXISTENT, INSISTENT; but note RESISTANT.

70. secondary (12). If it's an adjective, it probably ends in -ary.

71. liquefy (18). One of the few -efy words. The noun form is LIQUE-FACTION. Other words of this form are PUTREFY, RAREFY, and STUPEFY.

72. beautification (5, 18). Many -ify verbs have this noun form: AM-PLIFICATION, MAGNIFICATION, CERTIFICATION, etc.

73. weird (8). See No. 52, SEIZE.

74. erroneous (15). One of the relatively few -eous words.

75. heroes (6). But compare the rhyming word ZEROS.

76. embroidery (12). Most nouns end in -ery; most adjectives end in -ary. Compare a STATIONERY store and a STATIONARY location.

77. definite (1). Compare FINITE, INFINITE.

78. apologize (14). The list of -ize words is almost endless and still growing.

79. predictable (11, 13). Remember that if the basic word is found within the longer word, the ending is probably -able. Compare ACCEPT-ABLE, DEPENDABLE, FAVORABLE.

80. advertise (14). This is in the group of twenty or so -ise words. Most of the others end in -ize.

81. benefited (3). There is only one t because the main accent is on another syllable.

82. precede (20). Compare PROCEED and PROCEDURE.

83. mischievous (15). If you spelled this with -ious, check your pro-nunciation.

84. phenomena (6). Note also CRITERION, CRITERIA; GANGLION, GANGLIA.

85. supersede (11, 20). Did you remember that this is the only –sede word?

86. focuses (3, 6). Do not double the s̲, because the accent is on the first syllable.

87. society (8). Note also NOTORIETY, SOBRIETY, PIETY, VARIETY.

88. succeed (20). You can hear both c̲'s. Do you remember the other two –ceed words?

89. preference (3, 11, 17). No double letters in this word.

90. women's (10). The standard 's̲ for the possessive.

91. piteous (5, 15). This is an exception to the usual "y̲ to i̲" rule. Note also BEAUTEOUS, BOUNTEOUS, PLENTEOUS.

92. M.D.'s (6). Use 's̲ for plurals of abbreviations.

93. coolly (3). You can hear both l̲'s in this word. A similar word, COOLY, is usually spelled COOLIE and means a laborer.

94. patience (9, 17). Other words with ti̲ to indicate the sh̲ sound are SPATIAL, PALATIAL.

95. iridescent (11, 17). Only one r̲. Only one of the –escent words in Chapter 17 has a double letter: EFFERVESCENT.

96. regret (1). The e̲ in the second syllable is short, so there is no silent e̲.

97. conversion (16). Compare REVERT, REVERSION; PERVERT, PER-VERSION; SUBVERT, SUBVERSION; INVERT, INVERSION.

98. tariffs (6). Simply add s̲ to form the plural of any word ending in double f̲.

99. receipt (8). Watch that silent p̲ and compare RECEIVE.

100. livelihood (2, 5). Be careful with that –li when you add another ending. Compare LIKELIHOOD, MANLINESS, LONELIER.

Part Four

The pressure is off in this part. You might regard these supplementary chapters as a bonus for highly motivated students, good spellers (even the best spellers run into occasional problems), and word lovers.

The chapters in Part 4 are unprogrammed, although exercises are included to help you check your understanding of the material. They can be read in any order, so you can use them as you choose. This part includes chapters on these special problem areas:

- words commonly misspelled because they are mispronounced;

- words with silent initial letters;

- sound-alikes whose spellings are often confused;

- French words commonly used in English;

- German words commonly used in English;

- Spanish words commonly used in English.

The chapters describe and list the main problem words in the special areas listed above and give you practice in correctly spelling some of them. However, because the range of problems is so broad, no special rules or guidelines are available for individual words. It is also impossible to include exercises for all of them.

You can make use of the chapters by reading through the word lists carefully, doing the exercises, and checking off those words that are problems for you. To test your mastery of the words in this section, you might ask a friend to read all of the words aloud as you write them. Your friend might learn something, too! You may also find the supplementary chapters useful for later reference.

SUPPLEMENT 1

Foiled by Mispronunciation

Even if you pronounce most words correctly, you cannot spell a word correctly from sound alone. However, there is a long list of words in English that are so commonly mispronounced that there is little hope of setting them down correctly on paper. A striking example of this is the word PRONUNCIATION itself, which is often pronounced as if it were spelled PRONOUNCIATION. In this case, and in many others, there is a change in the spelling of a portion of the word when the form is changed from verb to noun. The verb is PRONOUNCE; the noun is PRONUNCIATION.

The dictionary reflects popular usage, but the process by which a spelling change, stemming from a change in pronunciation, gets into the dictionary is slow. If the common mispronunciation (and misspelling) of that cold region to the north continues to spread, the dictionary will eventually have to show the word as ARTIC (it's really ARCTIC), but that day has not yet come, and the word is commonly misspelled as shown.

Sometimes the reason for an incorrect pronunciation is simply the human habit of slurring over certain sounds until they drop out altogether. Some mispronunciations (with resulting misspellings) are caused by the force of analogy. Hundreds of words relating to specialized sciences end with -ology (for example, PSYCHOLOGY, BIOLOGY, and GEOLOGY). It is not surprising that the average person is driven by his experience with all those words to mispronounce—and misspell—the two common exceptions: GENEALOGY and MINERALOGY. Even these two words are not true exceptions if you consider that one of them comes from the old Greek word genea, which means "descent," and the other is simply derived from MINERAL. Thus, study these three—ANALOGY, GENEALOGY, and MINERALOGY—and don't worry about the others. All the others end in -ology, although there might be other things about them to give you trouble.

Some words are mispronounced because of association with other words. A prime example of this is SACRILEGIOUS. Since the word is closely associated with things RELIGIOUS, it is no wonder that the common misspelling is SACRELIGIOUS. However, the word is actually the

176

adjective form of SACRILEGE.

    The following list includes a good many words that are misspelled because they are mispronounced. (No list could possibly include them all.) If the misspelling is caused by slurred letters or if the error is caused by the insertion of a letter or some other common mispronunciation, that part of the word is underlined.

accessory

accidentally

appropriate

arctic

arithmetic

aspirin

asterisk

athlete

athletic

auxiliary

bankruptcy

boundary

brethren

candidate

cauliflower

children

chimney

chocolate

column

compliment*

cruel

diabetes

diary

disastrous

escape

extraordinary

February

fluorescent

fluoridate

gabardine

genealogy

government

grievous

guillotine

handkerchief

height

heinous

help

hiatus

hundred

incidentally

incongruous

intravenous

jewel

kindergarten

laboratory

laundry

length

liaison

library

licorice

literature

logarithm

lustrous

mathematics

mineralogy

miniature

minuscule

mischievous

modern

monstrous

okra

pabulum

paraphernalia

perspiration

perspire

poem

poetry

poinsettia

pomegranate

prerequisite

prerogative

prescribe

prescription

privilege

probably

pronunciation

reminisce

reminiscent

ruin

sacrilegious

sarsaparilla

sherbet

sophomore

subpoena

superfluous

superintendent

tarpaulin

temperament

temperature

told

veterinary

violence

violet

---

*Or complement. See Supplement 3.

Circle each misspelled word in the following paragraph and write the correct spelling.

The chemist's experiment proved to be disasterous when
he tried to use the new bleach formula in labortory tests.
Having selected a pile of laundery soiled with choclate,
licorish, and prespiration stains, he adjusted the water
temperture and added the bleach. But he was careless,
and what he thought was bleach was actually hydrochloric
acid!

— — — — — — — — — — — — — —

disastrous, laboratory, laundry, chocolate, licorice, perspiration,
temperature

SUPPLEMENT 2
Silent Beginnings

A fairly large number of words in English begin with a silent consonant. Many of these are of little interest to the general reading (and spelling) public because they are scientific words that are rarely used except by the experts. Such a word is CTENOPHORE, which means a marine, jellyfishlike animal. Unless you happen to be a marine biologist, this word probably holds little interest for you.

The silent letters that commonly begin words in English are g, h, k, m, p, and w. The main words beginning with silent g are:

gnarl	gnaw	gnomon
gnash	gneiss	gnomonic
gnat	gnome	gnosis
gnathic	gnomic	gnostic
gnathonic	gnomology	gnu

Most people spend their whole lives without the need to spell more than six of the fifteen words in the above list.

The silent h is considerably more common in England than in the United States. The h is now sounded in many words where formerly it was silent. For example, the transition from the unsounded to the sounded initial letter is apparent in the common phrase, "an historic occasion." Most Americans sound the h in HISTORIC, although some still precede the word with AN rather than A. There are six basic words related to HONOR on the list of silent h words, and only four others in common use:

heir	honesty	honorary
heiress	honor	honorific
herb	honorable	hour
honest	honorarium	

Many of the silent k̲ words are from German, a language closely related to English. The k̲ was originally pronounced (just as it still is in
the Scandinavian languages and German), but it eventually dropped out of
English. Here are the main words beginning with a silent k̲:

knack	knew	knock
knapsack	Knickerbocker	knoll
knave	knickers	knot
knead	knife	know
knee	knight	knowledge
kneel	knit	knuckle
knell	knob	

Sometimes a mnemonic device (memory aid) is used to help with a
difficult word. "Two robbers from Sing Sing," for example, is a phrase
that will help you remember that EMBARRASS has two r̲'s and two s̲'s.
Mnemonics is the art of improving memory. (Now you have been exposed
to the only basic word in common use that begins with silent m̲.)
    Silent p̲ is usually followed by n̲, s̲, or t̲. The main words in this
group are:

pneumatic	psychiatrist	psychoneurosis
pneumonia	psychiatry	psychopath
psalm	psychic	psychosis
psalmist	psychoanalysis	psychotic
Psalter	psychodynamic	psychosomatic
pseudonym	psychogenic	psychrometer
pseudopod	psychological	ptarmigan
psittacosis	psychology	pterodactyl
psyche	psychometry	Ptolemy
psychiatric	psychomotor	ptomaine

Despite the length of the silent p̲ words, they are not really difficult
if you break them down into their component parts. One of the longest
words on the list is a word you might occasionally use, and you encounter
it frequently because of the current interest in emotional and mental
health. PSYCHOANALYSIS is merely PSYCHO- plus ANALYSIS. Broken
all the way down into syllables, it is PSY-CHO-A-NAL-Y-SIS. Try
doing the same thing with PSITTACOSIS or PTERODACTYL, and you will
have more confidence in dealing with these words.
    Most of the words starting with silent w̲, having been around since the
very beginnings of English, are common words. Words beginning with
wh̲ are not included in the following list because they are mostly very
common, everyday words such as WHO, WHAT, WHEN, WHERE, and
WHY. In fact, most words beginning with wh̲ are not even examples of
silent initial letters because the wh̲ is a combined sound that is not like
either w̲ or h̲.

The main words that begin with silent w are:

wrack	wren	wrinkle
wraith	wrench	wrist
wrangle	wrest	writ
wrap	wrestle	write
wrath	wretch	writhe
wreak	wriggle	wrong
wreath	wright*	wrought
wreck	wring	wry

EXERCISE

Circle each word that is misspelled and write the correct spelling in the space beside it.

1. gnat _____   7. restle _____

2. gnee _____   8. wreath _____

3. neumonia _____   9. gnave _____

4. psychic _____   10. kneel _____

5. onor _____   11. herb _____

6. knaw _____   12. knife _____

- - - - - - - - - - - - - -

   2. knee; 3. pneumonia; 5. honor; 6. gnaw; 7. wrestle; 9. knave

*Usually in combinations such as SHIPWRIGHT and MILLWRIGHT.

Troublesome Twins

Many pairs of English words are not particularly hard to spell, but they are confusing because they sound somewhat alike. In a few cases, one of the words is mispronounced so that it resembles the other word, so the problem is which one to use in a given situation.

The following list of commonly confused pairs of words is by no means all-inclusive. The word or phrase in parentheses after each word is not intended to be an accurate definition (use your dictionary for that), but is merely a clue to help you choose the word you want.

This chapter includes a pre-test before the word list and an exercise at the end of the chapter. Try the pre-test to see how well you can distinguish between "troublesome twins." Answers to the pre-test are included, but it will be more useful to you if you mentally check your own answers as you read through the word list following the pre-test.

PRE-TEST

Match each word on the left with a definition.

_____	1. altar	(a)	tough fabric
_____	2. borne	(b)	in great need
_____	3. canvas	(c)	item of church furniture
_____	4. croquette	(d)	migrant coming in
_____	5. desperate	(e)	weaponry
_____	6. immigrant	(f)	painful
_____	7. lightning	(g)	in one place
_____	8. ordnance	(h)	electric flash
_____	9. stationary	(i)	carried
_____	10. torturous	(j)	kind of food
_____	11. alter	(k)	making lighter
_____	12. born	(l)	change
_____	13. canvass	(m)	take a poll
_____	14. croquet	(n)	different
_____	15. disparate	(o)	law
_____	16. emigrant	(p)	paper
_____	17. lightening	(q)	twisting
_____	18. ordinance	(r)	brought into being
_____	19. stationery	(s)	game
_____	20. tortuous	(t)	migrant going out

- - - - - - - - - - - - - - -

The answers are given below, but don't check them yet. Read through the word list, check (and possibly change) your answers, and <u>then</u> compare your answers with the ones given below.

1. c; 2. i; 3. a; 4. j; 5. b; 6. d; 7. h; 8. e; 9. g; 10. f;
11. l; 12. r; 13. m; 14. s; 15. n; 16. t; 17. k; 18. o;
19. p; 20. q

TROUBLESOME TWINS

Many of the words in the following list are marked with an asterisk (*) to show that the spelling confusion occurs because that word is mispronounced. NAIVE sounds nothing like KNAVE or NAVE, for example. You might have to use the dictionary to clarify some of these words.

adapt (adjust)
adept (skilled)

adverse (hostile)
averse (unwilling)

advice (guidance)
advise (give counsel)

allay* (calm)
alley (lane)

allusion (reference)
illusion (deceptive appearance)

allude (refer to)
elude (escape)

altar (church furniture)
alter (change)

angel (spirit)
angle (geometry term)

arc (curve)
ark (Noah's boat)
arch* (curved structure)

ascent (going up)
assent (agreement)

bail (bucket handle; to empty
    water; security)
bale (bundle)

ball (dance; round object)
bawl (cry)

balm (ointment)
bomb (explosive)

bard (poet)
barred (prevented)

bare (uncovered)
bear (animal; to carry; to endure)

barren (empty)
baron (a nobleman)

base (foundation; lowly)
bass (low-pitched sound)

bate (lessen)
bait (lure)

bazaar (market)
bizarre (odd)

beach (seashore)
beech (tree)

beer (beverage)
bier (coffin base)

berth (bunk)
birth (baby)

boar (swine)
Boer (South African of Dutch
    descent)
boor (vulgar person)
bore (dull person; to drill;
    carried)

boarder (eats at a boarding
    house)
border (boundary)

bolder (braver)
boulder (large rock)

bootee (footwear for a baby)
booty (plunder)

born (brought into being)
borne (carried)

borough (town)
burro (pack animal)
burrow (hole; to excavate)
borrow (get a loan)

bough (branch)
bow (front of a ship; bend at
   the waist)

bouillon (soup)
bullion (gold or silver)

bow (weapon; knot)
beau (boyfriend)

braise (cook)
braze (solder)

brake (slow down)
break (damage, destroy)

breach (gap; violation)
breech (rear)

bread (food)
bred (produced)

breadth (width)
breath (air breathed)

brews (makes a beverage)
bruise (injury)

bridal (wedding)
bridle (harness)

broach (open a discussion)
brooch (jewelry)

burley (tobacco)
burly (muscular)

call (summon)
caul (membrane)

callous (unfeeling)
callus (thickening on skin)

cannon (artillery)
canon (law; church official)

canter (gallop)
cantor (singer)

canvas (fabric)
canvass (solicit; take a poll)

capital (wealth; official town)
capitol (legislative building)

carat (unit of weight)
carrot (vegetable)
caret (editor's mark)

carton (box)
cartoon (drawing)

casino (gambling place)
cassino (card game)

cast (actors; mold; throw)
caste (social class)

censor (examiner)
censer (used with incense)
censure (blame)

cession (act of ceding)
session (meeting)

chased (pursued)
chaste (pure)

chic* (stylish)
chick (baby bird)

chili (food)
chilly (cold)
Chile (country)

chord (music term)
cord (string)

cite (quote)
site (place)
sight (vision)

click (noise)
clique (small group)

climactic (from climax)
climatic (from climate)

clothes (apparel)
cloths (fabrics)

coarse (rough)
course (route, plan of study)

collision (crash)
collusion (fraud)

coma (trance)
comma (punctuation)

complacent (self-satisfied)
complaisant (obliging)

complement (balance)
compliment (flatter)

confidant* (trusted male friend)
confidante* (trusted female friend)
confident (sure)

conscience (voice within)
conscious (aware)

consul (diplomat)
council (meeting)
counsel (advice)

coral (sea formation)
corral* (animal enclosure)

coarse (rough)
course (plan of study)

creak (noise)
creek (stream)

creep (crawl)
crêpe* (fabric)

croquet* (game)
croquette (food)

cubical (cube-shaped)
cubicle (small room)

currant (raisin)
current (flow; timely)

dam (barrier)
damn (condemn)

demur (object)
demure (shy)

depravation (corruption)
deprivation (act of depriving)

deprecate* (disapprove)
depreciate (lose value)

descent (lineage; going down)
dissent (disagreement)

desert (abandon; dry region)
dessert (sweet food)

desperate (in great need)
disparate (different)

device (means; gadget)
devise (invent)

dinghy* (small boat)
dingy (dirty)

disburse (pay out)
disperse (scatter)

discomfit (cause trouble)
discomfort (mild distress)

discreet (prudent)
discrete (separate)

discus (disk)
discuss (talk over)

disillusion (free from illusion)
dissolution (dissolving)

divers (several; those who dive)
diverse (different)

dyeing (coloring)
dying (ceasing to live)

elicit (bring out)
illicit (illegal)

emigrant (migrant going out)
immigrant (migrant coming in)

eminent (prominent)
imminent (impending)

envelop (enfold)
envelope (letter wrapper)

epic (heroic tale)
epoch (era)

epitaph (tombstone inscription)
epithet (descriptive phrase)

exceed (surpass)
accede (agree)

exercise (drill)
exorcise (drive out demons)

extant (existing)
extent (degree)

faint (weak)
feint (pretense)

fair (unbiased; light-skinned)
fare (price; food)

faker (phony)
fakir (mystic; ascetic)

feat (deed)
feet (body part)
fete* (festival)

fiancé (engaged man)
fiancée (engaged woman)

fir (tree)
fur (animal hair)

fisher (one who fishes)
fissure (cleft)

flair (talent)
flare (blaze)

flea (insect)
flee (run away)

flew (did fly)
flue (chimney part)
flu (influenza)

forego (precede)
forgo (abstain)

fort (defended place)
forte (strong point)

foul (offensive)
fowl (bird)

funeral (burial rite)
funereal (dismal)

furry (hairy)
fury (rage)

gait (manner of moving)
gate (fence opening)

gamble (make bets)
gambol (frolic)

gild (plate with gold)
guild (organization)

gilt (gold-plated)
guilt (blame)

glacier (mass of ice)
glazier (glass cutter)

gorilla (ape)
guerrilla (warfare)

goulash* (stew)
galosh (boot)

grate (to scrape; bars)
great (large; famous)

grip (grasp)
grippe (flu)

grisly (gruesome)
grizzly (bear)

groan (moan)
grown (adult)

hail (icy pellets; salute)
hale (healthy)

hall (corridor; large room)
haul (pull; take away)

handsome (good-looking)
hansom (vehicle)

hangar (for aircraft)
hanger (for clothing)

heal (cure)
heel (part of foot)

heroin (drug)
heroine (heroic woman)

hoard (save)
horde (mob)

hostel (lodging)
hostile (ill-willed)

human (of man)
humane* (kind)

hurdle (barrier)
hurtle (rush)

hypercritical* (overly critical)
hypocritical (insincere)

idle (not busy)
idol (religious image)

impetuous (impulsive)
impetus* (moving force)

incite (provoke)
insight (understanding)

innervate (invigorate)
innovate (introduce a change)
enervate (weaken)

inflection (voice change)
infliction (suffering; punishment)
affliction (ailment)

ingenious (clever)
ingenuous (naive)

its (possessive)
it's (it is)

jam (fruit preserves)
jamb (side of door)

jester (clown)
gesture (expressive movement)

jinks (frolic)
jinx (curse)

juggler (performer)
jugular* (vein)

kill (slay)
kiln (oven)

knave (tricky fellow)
nave (part of church)
naïve* (unsophisticated)

lain (form of lie)
lane (road)

lama (priest)
llama (beast)

lame (crippled)
lame* (fabric)

lath (strip of wood)
lathe (machine)

leach (percolate)
leech (blood sucker)

lead (metal)
led (past tense of lead)

leak (hole)
leek (plant)

lei (flower necklace)
lay (lie)

lessen (make less)
lesson (instruction)

lesser (smaller)
lessor (one who leases)

levee (dike)
levy (collect)

liable (responsible)
libel (published harm)

liar (teller of lies)
lyre (musical instrument)

lightening (making lighter)
lightning (electric flash)

linage* (line count)
lineage (ancestry)

lineament (feature)
liniment (tonic for pain)

liqueur* (sweet liquor)
liquor (alcoholic drink)

liter* (liquid measure)
litter (rubbish; stretcher)

load (burden)
lode (mineral deposit)

loan (something lent)
lone (solitary)

loath (reluctant)
loathe (hate)

local (not widespread)
locale* (area)

loose (free)
lose (suffer loss)

loot (booty)
lute (musical instrument)

lumbar (lower back)
lumber (wood)

lye (caustic soda)
lie (recline; tell untruth)

magnate (tycoon)
magnet (that which attracts)

maize (corn)
maze (labyrinth)

manner (method)
manor (estate)

mantel (shelf)
mantle (cloak)

marital (pertaining to marriage)
martial (pertaining to war)
marshal (law officer; gather
   together)

marten (animal)
martin (bird)

material (substance)
materiel* (supplies)

may be (may happen)
maybe (perhaps)

mean (to signify; lowly; cruel)
mien (demeanor)

meat (food)
meet (encounter)
mete (measure out)

medal (award)
meddle (to interfere)
metal (substance)
mettle (spirit)

might (may; strength)
mite (bit; parasite)

mil (thousandth)
mill (factory)

milestone (marker)
millstone (rock)

miner (one who mines)
minor (lesser; under age)

missal (prayer book)
missile (weapon)

moose (animal)
mousse (pudding)

moral (ethical; lesson)
morale* (spirit)

morning (before noon)
mourning (grief)

mouse (rodent)
mousse* (pudding)

muscle (body part)
mussel (shell fish)

mustard (spice)
mustered (assembled)

naval (navy)
navel (belly button)

nay (no)
neigh (horse cry)

nougat (candy)
nugget (lump of gold)

nozzle (spout)
nuzzle (rub with nose)

oar (boat paddle)
ore (contains metal)

ocher (color)
okra (vegetable)

ordinance (law)
ordnance (weaponry)

oscillate (swing back and forth)
osculate (kiss)

packed (packaged)
pact (agreement)

paean (song of praise)
peon (peasant)

pail (bucket)
pale (lacking color)

pain (suffering)
pane (panel)

palate (mouth part)
pallet (bed; base)

parlay (betting term)
parley (conference)

partition* (divide)
petition (plea)

pastoral (rural)
pastorale* (music term)

peace (harmony)
piece (part)

peak (summit)
pique (arouse)
pique* (fabric)

pearl (jewel)
purl (knitting term)

peer (look; equal)
pier (dock)

pendant (ornament)
pendent (suspended)

penance (atonement)
pennants (banners)

perspective (view)
prospective (expected)

physic (medicine)
physique* (body)
physics (science)

pistil (flower part)
pistol (gun)

plum (fruit)
plumb (vertical)

pole (rod)
poll (survey)

populace (people)
populous (crowded)

pore (study; skin opening)
pour (flow)
poor (not rich)

pray (make prayer)
prey (victim)

precede (go before)
proceed (go ahead; continue)

precedence (priority)
precedents (prior examples)
presidents (heads of government)

precis* (summary)
precise (exact)

premier (chief)
premiere (debut)

prescribe* (order)
proscribe (forbid)

principal (chief)
principle (rule)

profit (gain)
prophet (seer)

prophecy
prophesy* (tell the future)

prostate (gland)
prostrate (lying flat)

quarts (measure)
quartz (mineral)

rain (water)
reign (rule)

raise (lift)
raze (destroy)

rapped (knocked)
rapt (engrossed)

rational (reasonable)
rationale* (basis)

real (actual)
reel (spool; stagger; dance)

receipt (written acknowledgment)
recipe* (cooking instructions)

refuge (shelter)
refugee (seeker of shelter)

regal (royal)
regale* (amuse)

rest (repose)
wrest (twist violently)

resume (start again)
résumé* (summary)

reverend (clergyman)
reverent (respectful)

review (study again)
revue (entertainment)

rhyme (verse)
rime (ice)

riffle (shuffle)
rifle (firearm)

right (correct)
rite (ceremony)

risky (dangerous)
risqué* (naughty)

roe (fish eggs)
row (line)

role (part played)
roll (turn; bread)

roomer (lodger)
rumor (gossip)

rough (irregular)
ruff (neckpiece)

rout (drive out)
route (road)

rung (past of ring; ladder step)
wrung (past of wring)

rye (grain)
wry (distorted)

sac (pouch in plant or animal)
sack (large bag)

salon (shop; large room)
saloon (tavern)

scrip (paper money)
script (test; writing)

sculptor (artist)
sculpture (work of art)

sear (burn)
sere (dry)
seer (fortune teller)

secret (hidden)
secrete* (hide; give off)

serf (peasant)
surf (waves)

session (meeting)
cession (act of ceding)

shear (cut)
sheer (utter; transparent)

sheik (chief)
chic (stylish)

shudder (tremble)
shutter (screen)

sing (make a song)
singe* (burn)

slay (kill)
sleigh (sled)

sleight (skill; trick)
slight (discourtesy; slim)

slew (killed; many)
slough* (swamp)

soar (fly)
sore (hurting)

solder* (make connection)
soldier (warrior)

some (a few)
sum (quantity)

soul (spirit)
sole (foot part; only; fish)

staid (sedate)
stayed (past of stay)

stair (step)
stare (look at)

stationary (in one place)
stationery (paper)

steak (meat)
stake (post; bet)

step (walk; stair)
steppe (plain)

straight (not curved)
strait (situation; body of water)

striped* (has stripes)
stripped (removed)

suburb (city outskirts)
superb (excellent)

suit* (clothing)
suite (rooms; set of furniture)
sweet (sugary)

surely (certainly)
surly (rude)

surge (a swelling)
serge (cloth)

symbol (sign)
cymbal (percussion instrument)

tartar (acid; sauce)
tartare* (steak)

taught (did teach)
taut (tight)

tenant (dweller)
tenet (doctrine)

throe (spasm)
throw (pitch)

tic (twitch)
tick (parasite; sound; mattress)

tier (row)
tear (drop of water from eye)

tortuous* (twisting)
torturous (painful)

troop (soldiers)
troupe (actors)

trustee* (administrator)
trusty (reliable; trusted inmate)

turn (revolve)
tern (sea bird)

vale (valley)
veil (obscuring fabric)

vain (futile; conceited)
vane (flat surface)
vein (channel; streak; blood vessel)

vial (container)
vile (repulsive)

waive (forgo)
wave (moving water)

waiver (permitted exception)
waver (vacillate)

weather (climate)
whether (if)

while (during)
wile (trick)

wright (worker)
write (scribble)
right (correct)
rite (ceremony)

EXERCISES

Match each word on the left with a definition.

____ 1. coma	(a) weaken
____ 2. dingy	(b) small boat
____ 3. course	(c) housing for aircraft
____ 4. hangar	(d) meeting
____ 5. enervate	(e) plan of study
____ 6. metal	(f) labyrinth
____ 7. session	(g) invigorate
____ 8. maze	(h) act of ceding
____ 9. pendant	(i) hanging
____ 10. martial	(j) state of unconsciousness
____ 11. comma	(k) dirty
____ 12. hanger	(l) punctuation
____ 13. innervate	(m) corn
____ 14. maize	(n) for hanging clothes
____ 15. cession	(o) pertaining to war
____ 16. mettle	(p) law officer
____ 17. marshal	(q) such as iron
____ 18. coarse	(r) ornament
____ 19. dinghy	(s) spirit
____ 20. pendent	(t) rough

- - - - - - - - - - - - -

1. j; 2. k; 3. e; 4. c; 5. a; 6. q; 7. d; 8. f; 9. r; 10. o;
11. l; 12. n; 13. g; 14. m; 15. h; 16. s; 17. p; 18. t;
19. b; 20. i

Fill in the blanks with the appropriate words.

1. Greeley's ad_____ to the adventurous was, "Go west, young man."

2. The fox tried in vain to _____lude his pursuers.

3. Many scientists watched the as_____ of the rocket.

4. His conversation marked him as a bo_____, and his conduct convinced his companions that he was also a bo_____.

5. The park was crisscrossed with br_____ paths.

6. The burl_____ stevedore could lift incredible loads.

7. The capit_____ building was located in the most beautiful part of the capit_____ city.

8. The marriage of priests of the Latin rite is forbidden by can_____ law.

9. The young girl blushed when her boyfriend paid her a compl_____.

10. His office was little more than a small cub_____.

- - - - - - - - - - - - - - -

1. advice; 2. elude; 3. ascent; 4. bore, boor; 5. bridle; 6. burly; 7. capitol, capital; 8. canon; 9. compliment; 10. cubicle

Fill in the blanks with the appropriate words.

1. A cu_____ is a kind of raisin.

2. To dev_____ something new is to inno_____.

3. The computer program involved 32 discr_____ steps.

4. He was condemned for his _____icit romance.

5. The unruly crowd was ordered to dis_____se.

6. The smog threatened to envel_____ the whole city.

7. The young man's fianc_____ was extremely attractive.

8. The actions of the Pharisees were often hyp_____tical.

9. The proud matron traced her lin_____ge back to Queen Victoria.

10. The people were loat_____ to forgive the senator's misdeeds.

11. A mant _____ is a kind of cloak.

12. A mart_____ is a bird, while a mart_____ is an animal.

13. The great aircraft carrier was prominent in nav_____ operations.

14. A fine wine is a delight to the pal_____.

15. The airplane was endangered by r_____(ice) on its wings.

- - - - - - - - - - - - - - -

1. currant; 2. devise, innovate; 3. discrete; 4. illicit; 5. disperse; 6. envelop; 7. fiancee; 8. hypocritical; 9. lineage; 10. loath; 11. mantle; 12. martin, marten; 13. naval; 14. palate; 15. rime

SUPPLEMENT 4

No Fun with the French

The English-speaking people have never been backward about adopting words from other languages. Take ENTREPRENEUR, for example, a word closely related to that solid American word ENTERPRISE. With the rise of capitalism came a need for a word to describe the man who risks his capital to provide goods or services to others (with some profit to himself). Since he undertakes to set the machinery of production in motion, it seemed reasonable to call him an undertaker. But the word UNDERTAKER was already in use to describe one engaged in a specialized and well-known enterprise. Thus the French for undertaker came intact into English as ENTREPRENEUR. Some other examples of French words that have come into English to fill specific needs are: DEBUT, CHEF, COMMUNIQUÉ, and LIAISON.

The number of French words in the English language is surprisingly large. The spelling remains unchanged, except for the occasional omission of an accent mark, and the pronunciation ranges from reasonably pure French to something that would be unrecognizable in Paris. One thing is certain about these words: They are spelling nightmares for many Americans.

Literature and even conversation are sprinkled with French phrases (PIÈCE DE RÉSISTANCE, TOUR DE FORCE, HORS D'OEUVRES). There is a valid need for some of them, simply because no precise English equivalent exists. Sometimes, of course, such expressions are used merely for show. Rather than saying someone has been rendered HORS DE COMBAT, it might be better just to say that he is out of action. But there are many respectable and even indispensable French words in English. The ones likely to be used by most people are given in the following list.

If you study the words given, you will probably discover certain spelling patterns, but there are plenty of pitfalls. When in doubt, always use the dictionary. In some cases, plurals are also given. Study the list and then try the exercise that follows.

amateur
beau, beaux
blasé
boudoir
bouillabaisse
bouillon
boulevard
bouquet
bourgeois
bourgeoisie
brassière
bric-a-brac
brochure
brunette
brusque
buffet
cabaret
camaraderie
camisole
camouflage
canapé
cantaloupe
caprice
carafe
cavalier
chaise
chalet
chamois
champagne
chandelier
chapeau,
   chapeaux
chaperon
chateau,
   chateaux
chartreuse
chauffeur
chef
chemise
chenille
chevalier
chic
chiffon
chignon
clairvoyance
claque
cliché

clique
coiffure
cologne
communiqué
connoisseur
consommé
coquette
corsage
courier
crepe
croquet
croquette
cuisine
débris
debut
debutante
décor
deluxe
devotee
dilettante
douche
éclair
facade
fiancé
fiancée
gigolo
gourmet
guillotine
impromptu
ingénue
lamé
lavaliere
liaison
lieu
lingerie
liqueur
lorgnette
macabre
massage
masseur
masseuse
mayonnaise
mélange
mêlée
memoir
ménage
menagerie

meringue
métier
milieu
naïve
naïveté
née
papier-mâché
parfait
parquet
passé
petite
piqué
pirouette
pompadour
potpourri
précis
premier
première
purée
raconteur
reconnaissance
reconnoiter
rendezvous
repertoire
reservoir
restaurant
restauranteur
résumé
réveille
risqué
roulette
sabotage
saboteur
sachet
sauté
sautéed
séance
silhouette
soufflé
suave
souvenir
tourniquet
travail
troupe
trousseau
   trousseaux

EXERCISE

Circle each misspelled word below and write the correct spelling in the space beside it.

1.	amateur	_____	17.	boullion	_____	
2.	brasiere	_____	18.	boulevard	_____	
3.	camoflauge	_____	19.	borgeois	_____	
4.	chaperone	_____	20.	choufeur	_____	
5.	chenille	_____	21.	debrie	_____	
6.	connoiseur	_____	22.	lingere	_____	
7.	dilettante	_____	23.	masseur	_____	
8.	guillotine	_____	24.	rendevous	_____	
9.	laison	_____	25.	revellie	_____	
10.	mayonaisse	_____	26.	saboteur	_____	
11.	reconaissance	_____	27.	memoire	_____	
12.	resevoir	_____	28.	debutante	_____	
13.	sabotage	_____	29.	chartruse	_____	
14.	silhuette	_____	30.	suave	_____	
15.	souvenir	_____	31.	cameraderie	_____	
16.	trousseau	_____	32.	milieu	_____	

– – – – – – – – – – – – – – –

2. brassiere; 3. camouflage; 4. chaperon; 6. connoisseur;
9. liaison; 10. mayonnaise; 11. reconnaissance; 12. reservoir;
14. silhouette; 17. bouillon; 19. bourgeois; 20. chauffeur;
21. debris; 22. lingerie; 24. rendezvous; 25. reveille;
27. memoir; 29. chartreuse; 31. camaraderie

SUPPLEMENT 5

Grappling with German

Many English words are closely related to the German of an earlier time, but few modern German words are commonly encountered in English. World War II brought a number of German words into such widespread use that they now appear in most dictionaries, but even so, there are only five words on our list that are used by almost all Americans: GESTAPO, KINDERGARTEN, NAZI, SAUERKRAUT, and "GESUNDHEIT!"

Don't be discouraged if some of the words on the following list are totally unfamiliar. They are of interest only in highly specialized fields (notably psychology) and are included for reference only. The word list shows each word as it is generally written in English. Study the list and then try the exercise that follows.

blitzkrieg	kindergarten	Reich
Bund	Junker	Reichstag
Das Kapital	lebensraum	sauerkraut
Fuehrer	Luftwaffe	verboten
Gestalt	lederhosen	Weltanschauung
Gestapo	Mein Kampf	Weltansicht
Gesundheit	Nazi	Weltpolitik
glockenspiel	Panzer	Weltschmerz
kaput	poltergeist	

EXERCISE

Each of the following words is misspelled. Write the correct spelling in the space beside it.

1. blitzkreig   _____

2. Fuhrer   _____

3. Gestappo   _____

4. gluckenspiel   _____

5. kintergarden   _____

6. liederhosen   _____

7. poultergeist   _____

8. sourkraut   _____

- - - - - - - - - - - - - -

1. blitzkrieg; 2. Fuehrer; 3. Gestapo; 4. glockenspiel; 5. kindergarten; 6. lederhosen; 7. poltergeist; 8. sauerkraut

SUPPLEMENT 6

Spelling in Spanish

Since Spanish is the language of Mexico and most points south, it is hardly surprising that a large number of words from the language have come unchanged into English. The western and southwestern states have large Spanish-speaking populations that have brought much of their native culture with them. More recently, New York City, Miami, and other metropolitan centers have felt the influence on the local language from the increasing numbers of Spanish-speaking people.

Most of the Spanish words on the following list are related to very basic aspects of life (such as food, clothing, and shelter). The list is growing as Americans become more internationally oriented. Study the list and then try the exercise that follows.

adobe	hacienda	serape
arroyo	mantilla	sombrero
barrio	matador	taco
bracero	mesa	tamale
chili con carne	rancho	tequila
condor	rodeo	tortilla
enchilada		

EXERCISE

Each of the following words is misspelled. Write the correct spelling in
the space beside it.

1. addobe   _____

2. aroyo   _____

3. brasero   _____

4. conder   _____

5. haciendo   _____

6. mantila   _____

7. rodio   _____

8. sombrerro   _____

9. tequilla   _____

— — — — — — — — — — — — — — —

1. adobe; 2. arroyo; 3. bracero; 4. condor; 5. hacienda;
6. mantilla; 7. rodeo; 8. sombrero; 9. tequila

SUPPLEMENT 7

Do-It-Yourself Memory Aids

Spelling guidelines are not much help with words like ANCHOVY, PAR-ALLEL, RECONNOITER, or FRICASSEE. If the word is unusual or sel-dom-used, there's always the dictionary. But if you really want to con-quer some of those words that keep coming up to plague you, you might give some thought to developing your own memory aids.

Memory is a strange thing; no one knows exactly how it works. It is clear, however, that certain mental exercises are effective in fixing the desired information in your memory. These exercises might be silly, illogical, humorous—it doesn't matter, as long as they work. And what works for you might not work for someone else.

You bring your own background, education, and personality to the task of developing a memory aid. For example, let's take ANCHOVY, a word to which spelling rules are not very applicable. Since an anchovy is a small, herringlike fish, you might start out with another word re-lated to the sea. ANCHOR is such a word, so a mental picture of an an-chovy clinging to an anchor helps you to get it started right. But you still need something to remind you that the ending is -vy and not -vey. An anchor is HEAVY, a word that ends in -vy. Put them together, and you have ANCHOVY. Of course if you're not careful, you might end up with "anchorvy," but you had to study the structure of the word to work out the memory aid, and the sound of r is not heard in ANCHOVY. Any-way, you're working out an aid to memory, not a guarantee! You will find, however, that the effort of merely trying to work out a memory aid will fix the correct spelling in your mind, since you have to concentrate on the spelling problem in the first place.

A common problem is doubled or undoubled consonants. Take the word ANOINT, which is commonly misspelled with a double n. Perhaps you can work out a phrase that includes all the letters of the problem word in the correct sequence. One such phrase is "ANOINT with an oint-ment." A similar problem word is ABANDON. You might remember it by thinking of "a band on her finger."

Another word with the problem of doubled or undoubled consonants is PARALLEL. Where is the double l? I might think, "All double l's are parallel," and remember the double l in all. You might try a different approach, but even if you can't think of a suitable memory aid, working on the problem often solves it.

APPROPRIATE is often mispronounced and therefore misspelled. A common tendency is to leave out the second r. To further complicate things, you might have trouble with the p's. You might (if your mind works that way) try to relate the meaning of the word to your spelling problems. APPROPRIATE means apt, proper, right. That sentence reminds me that there is a double p and then a single p, and that both pp and p are followed by r. It might not help you at all.

Sometimes the problem is not spelling but the confusion between sound-alikes. It's easy to confuse COMPLEMENT and COMPLIMENT. There are many approaches to the problem. You could consider the relationship between COMPLEMENT and SUPPLEMENT, if you happen to know how to spell SUPPLEMENT. You might remember that COMPLE-MENT means "make complete." Or you could work on the other word of the pair, thinking of something like "He plied her with compliments."

The main thing about developing memory aids to spelling is that you have to analyze the word, decide what the problem is, and then work to solve the problem. In trying to solve the problem, even when you think you fail, you focus attention on the word. Often that is enough.

APPENDIX
Some Special Word Lists

Every occupation and profession has its special vocabulary that includes many words not familiar to the general public.

Twenty-two lists of special terms are provided on the following pages for such use as you care to make of them. The lists are arranged in alphabetical order according to profession and include the following:

Accounting
Advertising, Printing, and Publishing
Agricultural
Automobile
Aviation
Banking and Investment
Building and Construction
Business and Commercial
Chemical
Civil Engineering
Drug
Electrical and Electronic
Government
Grocery and Food
Hardware
Insurance
Legal
Machinery
Medical
Musical
Real Estate
Transportation and Shipping

ACCOUNTING TERMS

account	contingent liability	liquid asset
account current	controlling account	net profit
administrative expense	credit	nominal account
amortization	creditor	obsolescence
assets	current asset	posting
auditor	debit	profit and loss statement
balance	debtor	proprietorship
balance sheet	fixed asset	reserve
book of original entry	footing	sinking fund
budget	good will	solvent
capital	imprest fund	subsidiary ledger
certified public accountant	intangible assets	tangible assets
closing the books	inventory	transaction
	journal	trial balance
	ledger	undivided profits
	liabilities	

ADVERTISING, PRINTING, AND PUBLISHING TERMS

addenda	die	manuscript
arabic figures	dummy	mat
Benday	electrotype	monotype
bibliography	emboss	octavo
by-line	engraving	offset
blurb	errata slip	pagination
boiler plate	folio	photogravure
boldface	font	pica
broadside	halftone	proofreader
brochure	house organ	quad
caption	italic	rotogravure
caret	layout	script
cartoon	leaders	slogan
colophon	linotype	stereotype
copyright	lithography	superior figure
copy writer	logotype	tear sheet
delete	lower case	woodcut

AGRICULTURAL TERMS

acreage	grazing	poultry
alluvial	greenhouse	prairie
brooder	harrow	reaper
citrus	hedge	rotation
creamery	horticulture	scythe
fallow	huckster	seepage
fertilizer	incubator	separator
fleece	insecticide	sheaves
fodder	irrigation	silage
forage	legume	spading
forestry	maize	stubble
fowl	meadow	stumpy
fungicide	motor plow	thresher
furrow	orchard	tractor
ginning	pasture	truck farm
grafting	plowshare	vehicle
granary		

AUTOMOBILE TERMS

accelerator	crankshaft	muffler
antifreeze	cylinder	packing
assembly	cylinder block	piston
axle	cylinder head	piston ring
bearing	defroster	propeller shaft
bore	differential	radiator
bushing	distributor	safety glass
cam	exhaust	sedan
camber	flywheel	shim
carburetor	gasket	speedometer
casing	gearshift	stroke
choke	generator	supercharger
clutch	governor	thermostat
compression ratio	horsepower	throttle
connecting rod	housing	toe-in
coupé	ignition	transmission
cowl	limousine	tread
crankcase	magneto	worm
crankpin	manifold	

AVIATION TERMS

aerodynamics
aeronautics
aerostat
aileron
airdrome
airfoil
altimeter
amphibian
autopilot
balloon
bank
blimp
catapult
ceiling
cockpit
control column

control stick
dirigible
elevator
fairing
fuselage
glider
ground loop
gyroscope
hangar
helicopter
instrument flying
landing gear
longeron
longitudinal
maneuverability

monoplane
multiengine
nacelle
needle and ball
omnirange
parachute
pilot tube
propeller
rudder
seaplane
stabilizer
stewardess
tachometer
visibility
wind tunnel

BANKING AND INVESTMENT TERMS

acceptance
accrued
appreciation
arbitrage
bearer
Big Board
bill of exchange
blue-sky laws
bond
broker
call money
canceled check
capital stock
cashier's check
certified check
check protector
clearinghouse
close corporation
collateral
commercial paper
commitment
common stock
comptroller

convertible
counter check
counterfeit
coupon
cumulative
currency
debenture
defalcation
denomination
deposit slip
depositor
depository
dishonor
diversification
dividend
draft
Federal Reserve
   Bank
fiduciary
forgery
futures
gilt-edged
greenback

hypothecation
indorse
inflation
investor
irredeemable
issue
joint account
legal tender
letter of credit
listed stocks
loan
margin
maturity
monetary
negotiable in-
   struments
no-par stock
nonassessable
odd lot
over the counter
overdraw
par value
passbook

BANKING AND INVESTMENT TERMS (continued)

payee	redemption	stub
point	right	teller
preferred stock	scrip	ticker
profit taking	seat	traveler's check
promissory note	security	usury
promoter	specie	utilities
protest	spot	vault
quotations	sterling	voucher check
rails	stock dividend	withdrawal
raise	stop-loss order	yield
reconciliation	stop payment	

BUILDING AND CONSTRUCTION TERMS

aisle	finial	masonry
alcove	flue	mortar
arcade	foyer	mortise
asphalt	gable	mosaic
balustrade	gargoyle	mullion
bas-relief	Gothic	mural
blueprint	grille	newel
bonding	jamb	niche
buttress	joists	panel
calcimine	keystone	patio
canopy	lacquer	pavilion
cantilever	lattice	proscenium
casement	lintel	rotunda
column	macadamize	specifications
cornice	mansard	stucco
corridor	mantel	transom
facade		

BUSINESS AND COMMERCIAL TERMS

account sales	allocation	assignment
accounts payable	allotment	back order
accounts receivable	apprentice	bankruptcy
acknowledgment	arbitration	barometer
advances	arrears	barter
agent	articles of agree-	bill of goods
agenda	ment	bonus

BUSINESS AND COMMERCIAL TERMS (continued)

boycott
break-even point
bylaws
by-product
calendar year
capitalization
cartage
certify
charter
client
clientele
collective bar-
    gaining
commission bro-
    ker
commodity
concession
conciliation
confirmation
consideration
consign
consolidate
consumer
corporation
cost plus
credentials
credit memoran-
    dum
custody
customs
cycle
cycle billing
decentralize
deductions
defaulter
depletion
deteriorate
director
disbursements
discount
discrepancy
discretionary
discrimination
document

domestic trade
drawing account
dun
dutiable goods
duty
efficiency
enterprise
equitable
escalator clause
establish
estimate
exchange
excise
exempt
expedite
exports
extension
facilities
financier
fiscal year
fixed charges
forecast
franchise
frank
fraudulent
freight
goods in process
gross profit
guarantee
holding company
imports
incorporated
infringement
inheritance
insolvency
installment
integrity
interlocking
investment
invoice
itemized state-
    ment
jobber
job evaluation

license
limited liability
line of credit
liquidation
lucrative
margin of pro-
    fit
marketability
mediation
mercantile agen-
    cy
merchandise
merger
middleman
minute book
monopoly
net
notary public
option
overhead
paper profits
partnership
patent
personal prop-
    erty
port of entry
postdated
potential
power of attor-
    ney
preferential
proceeds
prorate
prospectus
proxy
public utilities
purchase re-
    quisition
quota
rebate
recapitulation
recoup
redeemable
referee

BUSINESS AND COMMERCIAL TERMS (continued)

rescind
resources
retail
retrench
royalty
seniority
sight draft
substantial
sundries
surety
surplus

symbol
syndicate
tariff
terminology
testimonial
tracer
trade accept-
    ance
trade discount
trust

turnover
validity
verification
voucher
warehouse re-
    ceipt
wholesale
without recourse
workmen's com-
    pensation

CHEMICAL TERMS

aldehyde
alkali
amorphous
atomic
benzene
biochemistry
calcium
carbohydrate
cellulose
centigrade
chlorine
citrate
colloidal
crucible
crystalline
dioxide
effervesce
effloresce
enzyme
ester

ethylene
filtrate
fission
halogen
helium
homologous
hydrate
hydrochloride
iodide
ionize
isotope
litmus
mercury
metallurgy
monoxide
mordant
nascent
neutron
nitrate

nitrogen
nuclear physics
oxidation
phosphate
polymerization
potassium
protein
proton
radioactive
silicon
sodium
solvent
specific gravity
spectroscope
sulphur[*]
supersonic
uranium
vitriol
volatile

---

[*]Sometimes spelled SULFUR.

CIVIL ENGINEERING TERMS

abutment	elasticity	reservoir
aggregate	equilibrium	resilience
alignment	girder	rigidity
aqueduct	heterogeneous	rivet
artesian	homogeneous	sedimentation
caisson	hydraulic	segregation
centrifugal	hydroelectric	sewage
centripetal	hydrostatic	sewerage
compression	impermeable	siphon
conglomerate	lamination	surveyor
crevasse	lateral	tension
culvert	levee	torsion
diagonal	pneumatic	trestle
dowel	profile	turbine
ductile	reconnaissance	viaduct

DRUG TERMS

alcohol	dentifrice	mercurochrome
amphetamine	digitalis	merthiolate
ampoule	elixir	morphine
analgesic	emulsify	narcotic
anodyne	essence	nicotine
antacid	ether	oxygen
aperient	formaldehyde	paregoric
aromatic	gauze	penicillin
barbiturate	glycerin	pharmaceutical
belladonna	hashish	prescription
benzoin	heroin	procaine
bicarbonate	hormone	prophylactic
bismuth	insulin	quinine
caffeine	iodine	saccharin
camphor	iodoform	salve
capsule	lanolin	sedative
chloroform	lozenge	strychnine
cocaine	magnesia	tincture
codeine	marijuana	tranquilizer
collodion	menthol	vitamin

ELECTRICAL AND ELECTRONIC TERMS

alternating cur-
   rent
ammeter
ampere
amplifier
amplitude
anode
antenna
arc
armature
attenuation
battery
bias
capacitance
cathode
cathode ray tube
circuit
commutator
condenser
conductance
conductivity
conduit
continuity
controller
converter
coulomb
coupling
damping
decibel
deflection
demagnetization
detector
dielectric
diplex
direct current
distortion
dynamo
dynamometer

electrode
electrodynamics
electrolysis
electrolyte
electromagnet
electromotive
   force
electron
electron tube
farad
filament
filter
fluorescent
frequency
fuse
galvanoscope
Geiger counter
grid
hermetic
Hertz
heterodyne
hysteresis
impedance
incandescence
inductance
infrared
insulation
interference
kilocycle
kilowat
magnetomotive
megacycle
mho
microfarad
microphone
modulation
ohm

oscillator
ostillograph
permeability
photoelectric
picofared
piezoelectric
polarization
potentiometer
quartz crystal
radar
reactance
receiver
resistance
resonance
rheostat
selectivity
semiconductor
sensitivity
shunt
static
superheterodyne
synchronization
telephotograph
teletype
television
torque
transceiver
transformer
transistor
transmitter
tungsten
tuning
turbogenerator
vacuum tube
voltage
watt
wave length

GOVERNMENT TERMS

alien	diplomacy	parity
allies	documentary	parliament
ambassador	embassy	partisan
amendment	envoy	plenipotentiary
assessor	expatriate	precinct
attaché	federal	priority
autocracy	fusion	proletariat
bureaucracy	imperialism	propaganda
campaign	inauguration	protectorate
candidate	legation	protocol
censorship	legislature	quorum
civilian	lobbying	reactionary
conciliator	logrolling	reciprocity
constitutional	mandate	referendum
consulate	monarchy	republic
contraband	naturalization	senatorial
court-martial	neutrality	statism
customs	omnibus	suffrage
demagogue	opponent	unification
democracy	Pan-American	union

GROCERY AND FOOD TERMS

artichoke	coconut	oleomargarine
asparagus	consommé	pasteurizê
avocado	deviled	pâté de foie gras
banana	endive	piccalilli
barbecue	farina	pistachio
biscuit	hominy	pomegranate
bluing	kohlrabi	potpourri
bologna	kumquat	raisin
Brie cheese	lentils	rhubarb
broccoli	macaroni	Roquefort
canape	maraschino	sauerkraut
caviar	marjoram	syrup
cayenne	marron	sorghum
chili con carne	marshmallow	spaghetti
chop suey	matzoth	thyme
chowchow	mayonnaise	vermicelli
chow mein	mulligatawny	Zwieback
cocoa		

HARDWARE TERMS

andirons
asbestos
auger
carborundum
caster
chisel
chrome
cleaver
corrugated
currycomb
door check
emery
faucet
forceps
galvanized iron
gauge
gimlet

grindstone
handle
hinge
hoe
holster
hose
knob
knocker
ladle
latch
mattock
maul
nozzle
pail
pincers
pliers
plumb

putty
razor
reamer
scissors
screen
screw driver
sheeting
sickle
sieve
sledge
solder
tongs
trowel
twine
wedge
wrench
wringer

INSURANCE TERMS

actuarial
adjuster
annuity
appraiser
arson
attained age
beneficiary
blanket policy
burglary
cash-surrender
    value
casualty
claimant
commuted value
contingency
conversion
coverage

disability clause
employer's lia-
    bility
endowment
fidelity bond
forfeiture
fraternal
general average
indemnity
inflammable
insurable inter-
    est
lapse
Lloyd's of Lon-
    don
longevity
marine insurance

maritime
mortality
mutual
paid-up policy
peril
perpetuity
policyholder
premium
registrar
reinstate
rider
risk
social insurance
surrender value
survivor
tontine

LEGAL TERMS

abscond
acquittal
adjudicate
administrator
affidavit
alias
alimony
allegation
ambiguity
annulment
appellate
apprehend
appurtenance
assault
attachment
attestation
bailee
battery
bequeath
chancery
chattel
chose in action
clemency
codicil
decedent
decree
defendant
demise
demurrer
deponent
docket
domicile
duress
easement

embezzlement
eminent domain
equity
escrow
estoppel
executor
executrix
felony
garnishee
hereditaments
homicide
impanel
inchoate
incorporeal
indenture
injunction
intestate
judicial
jurisdiction
jurisprudence
larceny
legatee
lien
litigation
lunatic
malfeasance
mandamus
mandate
misdemeanor
mittimus
negligence
negotiate
nominal

outlawed
perjury
plaintiff
plea
probate
prosecute
quasi
ratification
residuary
restitution
revert
status
subpoena
subrogation
subscribe
summons
surrogate
tender
testator
testatrix
testimony
tort
trespass
trustee
ultra vires
unilateral
vagrancy
vendor
venire
venue
verdict
voidable
warrant

MACHINERY TERMS

abrasive	die	pinion
annealing	dovetail	pivot
anvil	eccentric	pneumatic
assemblage	flange	precision
axis	foundry	pulley
beams	friction	pumice
Bessemer	fusion	ratchet
blowtorch	gear	resiliency
brake	guy	rotor
burr	hoist	sheave
bushing	jack	smelting
cable	lever	sprocket
caliper	machinist	swivel
chain	malleable	template
chamfer	mandrel	tenon
chuck	mangle	tensile
combustion	manifold	trunnion
conveyer	mechanic	tumbler
corrosion	mold	vise
crane	pendulum	welded
cylindrical	periphery	wrought iron

MEDICAL TERMS

abdomen	astigmatism	contagious
abscess	atrophy	convalescence
acidosis	autointoxication	corpuscle
adenoid	autopsy	debility
adolescence	bacteria	delirious
alimentary	bandage	dermatologist
allergic	bronchitis	diabetes
amputation	capillary	diagnosis
anatomy	carbohydrate	diaphragm
anemia	carbuncle	diastolic
anesthetic	cardiac	diathermy
antibiotic	cardiogram	diphtheria
antiseptic	cartilage	dispensary
antitoxin	cerebral	dissect
aorta	chiropodist	enzyme
appendicitis	chiropractor	epidemic
appendix	chronic	epileptic
artery	clinical	esophagus
asthma	congenital	fluoroscope

MEDICAL TERMS (continued)

geriatrics	meningitis	podiatrist
germicide	metabolism	poliomyelitis
glandular	microbe	poultice
hemoglobin	microscope	prognosis
hemorrhage	migraine	prophylaxis
hiccup	morbidity	psychiatry
histamine	nasal	ptomaine
homeopathic	nausea	pulmonary
hospitalization	neuralgia	quarantine
hydrophobia	neurotic	radiothermy
hygiene	obese	respiratory
hypertension	organic	rheumatism
hypodermic	orthodontia	sanitarium
immunity	orthopedic	slerosis
infectious	osteopathy	serum
inflammation	pallor	stethoscope
inhibition	pancreas	surgeon
inoculation	paralysis	symptom
insomnia	paroxysm	thyroid
larynx	pediatrician	tonsillitis
lastex	pharynx	trachea
leukemia	physiotherapy	typhoid
malignant	phlegmatic	vaccine
mastoiditis	pneumonia	vertebra
melancholia		

MUSICAL TERMS

adagio	crescendo	opus
allegretto	diminuendo	oratorio
allegro	dissonance	orchestral
andante	encore	overture
andantino	forte	philharmonic
arpeggio	fortissimo	pianissimo
ballerina	fugue	prelude
ballet	glissando	prima ballerina
baritone	hymn	prima donna
baton	legato	rhapsody
chord	libretto	rhythm
choreography	metronome	scherzo
coloratura	minuet	sonata
concerto	obbligato	soprano
contralto	octave	staccato

MUSICAL TERMS (continued)

symphony	toccata	vivace
syncopation	virtuoso	waltz
tempo		

REAL ESTATE TERMS

abstract of title	encumbrance	mortgagee
appraisal	foreclosure	mortgagor
assessed valuation	frontage	occupancy
building and loan	lease	premises
association	lessee	realtor
conveyance	lessor	realty
dispossess	metes and	suburban
dower	bounds	tenant
ejectment	mortgage	zoning

TRANSPORTATION AND SHIPPING TERMS

air brake	derailment	passport
ballast	drayage	Pullman
bill of lading	embargo	refrigerator car
block signal	expressage	right of way
boatswain	fathom	roadbed
breakage	forecastle	route
bulkhead	freight	steerage
caboose	interstate	stevedore
carload	interurban	steward
classification	intrastate	stopover
commissary	itinerary	terminal
common carrier	jettison	timetable
commuter	locomotive	trainman
consignee	longshoreman	via
day coach	maintenance	waybill
demurrage	manifest	wharfage
depot		